FROM INSPIRATION TO INNOVATION

NATURE DESIGN

**EDITED BY
MUSEUM FÜR GESTALTUNG ZÜRICH
ANGELI SACHS**

Essays by Barry Bergdoll,
Dario Gamboni, and Philip Ursprung

LARS MÜLLER PUBLISHERS

Serge Hasenböhler, *Dendrocopus major,* **2007**
Lambda print, 115 × 90 cm
Serge Hasenböhler, Basel, CH.
Courtesy Galerie Gisèle Linder, Basel, CH

Serge Hasenböhler, *Passiflora ligularis,* **2007**
Lambda print, 115 × 90 cm
Serge Hasenböhler, Basel, CH.
Courtesy Galerie Gisèle Linder, Basel, CH

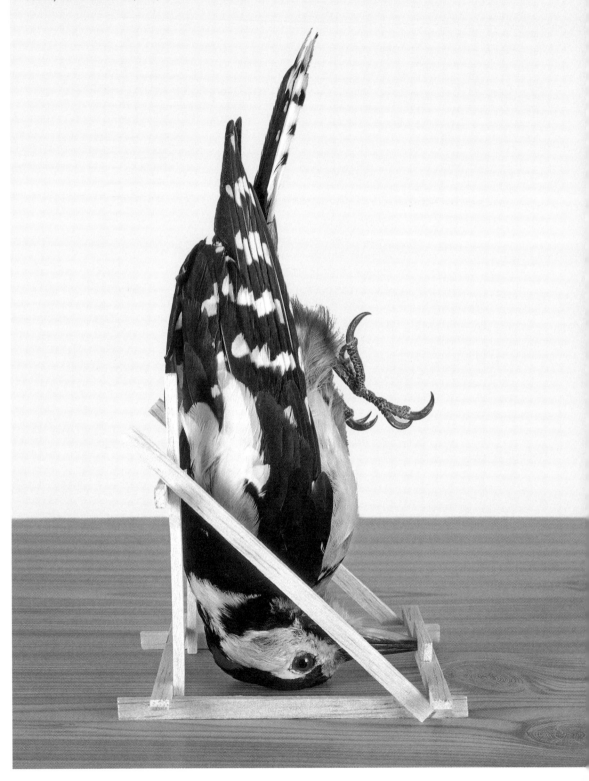

INTRODUCTION

Nature has been a constant source of inspiration in the design of the human environment, but one cannot help notice that the relationship between nature and the various design disciplines has in recent years intensified. The "model of nature," with its forms, structures, and organizing principles, does not only inspire the widest range of concepts and design processes, but also can be expressed in a broad spectrum of forms and functions. *Nature Design* refers to this phenomenon and presents an international selection of objects and projects from the fields of design, architecture, landscape architecture, art, photography, and scientific research, works that do not simply depict or imitate nature but use it as a starting point and reservoir of inspiration for eclectic and innovative responses to the relationship between man and his environment.

The book is divided into different sections: the historical and theoretical backgrounds of culminating moments in the relationship between nature and design from the eighteenth century until the present are exemplified in four "passages" and addressed in more detail in essays by Barry Bergdoll, Dario Gamboni, Philip Ursprung, and Angeli Sachs. They appear alternately with seven "thematic landscapes" in which the whole spectrum of the inspiration of nature and the concern with its processes can be seen. The thematic landscapes are: the sea with its flora and fauna, topographic concepts, the forms and materials of forests and of plants, anthropomorphic and zoomorphic approaches, scent, and climate.

In the first passage, "Discovering Nature," the basic principles for the overall project are laid out, and the history of our understanding of nature since the eighteenth century is illustrated through the important protagonists in the natural sciences and their works. The sequence begins with Maria Sibylla Merian, who with her examination and illustration of the metamorphoses of insects is the founder of entomology; it continues with Carl von Linné, who revolutionized the systemization and classification of nature with his *Systema Naturae*; Johann Wolfgang von Goethe's work as a morphologist; Charles Darwin, founder of the theory of evolution; the explorer and polymath Alexander von Humboldt up to Ernst Haeckel and his influential illustrations of *Radiolarien* (*Radiolaria*) and *Kunstformen der Natur* (*Art Forms of Nature*). In addition, the archiving, cataloguing, and systemization of nature is represented by preparations and models from botanical and zoological collections. With this as a foundation, there follows the artistic interpretation of nature, and that conveyed through the natural sciences by architects and artists such as John Ruskin, Henry van de Velde, and Bruno Taut from the mid-nineteenth century up to the 1920s.

Three further passages focus on culminating periods of nature's influence on modern design: Art Nouveau, in which the model of nature, especially the plant world and the dynamics of its growth, played a more influential role than in almost any other art movement; the 1930s to the 1970s, with its tendency towards organic design and technoid visions of the future; and contemporary design, inspired by various concepts of nature. Primarily represented here is a series of pioneering architecture projects that show distinctive contemporary interactions between nature and design.

In the thematic landscapes, the objects and projects from the history of twentieth-century design up to the present—culled from architecture, landscape architecture, and art—can be experienced as individual exhibits on the one hand, and, on the other, taken together they form a scenery in which the respective theme is presented in its various aspects. At the same time, a dialogue emerges between the more theoretical passages and the thematic landscapes, setting historical works and contemporary developments in context.

A number of artists, designers, architects, and landscape architects have developed works for *Nature Design* that respond to this concept and make complex contributions to the exhibition and the book. Serge Hasenböhler's bird, mounted in a three-dimensional frame and standing on its head, and its counterpart, a *passiflora* balancing on a frame, represent the starting point for the discovery of design inspired in nature from the past and the present, and the often complex questions arising from it. With *433 Eros*, Christian Waldvogel simulates the impact of an asteroid in the Zurich area as a "global scalpel." Werner Aisslinger builds a complex structure with mesh from high-tech cord which, with its honeycomb modules, is oriented on a zoomorphic construction and which simultaneously takes on the character of a canopy of leaves with its openings, aggregations, and overlaps. In *Yeux de Paon*, Olaf Nicolai follows the history of an ornament and its artificially contextualized use in mass production for tourists; with *Spiegel Nebel Wind* (Mirror, Fog, Wind) Günther Vogt concentrates on the phenomenon of nature; and with heat.seat, Jürgen Mayer H. transmits a completely new sense to temperature perception.

Other works of similar complexity are Yusuke Obuchi's Wave Garden, a project for a wave power station off the coast of California; Ines Schaber's and Jörg Stollmann's *On movers and shapers*, which illustrates how a gated community in the southwest United States defines its territory in the ideal desert landscape; Olafur Eliasson's *The Madagascar Hall series*, in which he marks the delimitations of the artificial paradise of the Masoala Rainforest Hall in Zurich; Lars Spuybroek's romantic renderings of his highly complex sculptures and buildings for public space; and Dominique Ghiggi's scent installation *Zavana* (Savannah), in which she conceives unused spaces of Zurich Airport as an imaginary African veldt landscape—symbolic of wilderness and freedom within the precisely defined specifications for the functionality of this facility of a globally-linked society. These contributions make an additional level of reading possible: they go into the themes in more detail and introduce critical questions.

Nature Design is intended to show the multiple possibilities in the rediscovery and reinvention of nature, and to open up new perspectives.

DISCOVERING NATURE

Research expeditions—such as those to the Americas—served as the foundation for the discovery of nature in the eighteenth and nineteenth centuries. The knowledge acquired through empirical research was integrated into the cataloguing and systematization of nature, or was expressed in models such as Charles Darwin's evolutionary tree of life.

The natural sciences and their popular interpretations, such as Ernst Haeckel's *Kunstformen der Natur*, influenced architecture and other design disciplines that absorbed motifs from nature and employed them artistically. Nature was no longer used only as ornament, but as a constituent element in the discovery of form.

Maria Sibylla Merian, *Metamorphosis Insectorum*
Surinamensium, **Amsterdam 1705. Plates VII and XI**
Illustrated book with 60 hand-colored copper plates, 53.5 × 36.5 cm
Museum für Gestaltung Zürich, Grafiksammlung

Maria Sibylla Merian is regarded as the true founder of
entomology (the study of insects). Though unusual for
the mid-seventeenth century, in her youth she had already
begun the systematic investigation of various insects,
the stages of their development, and their relationship
to the plants they eat. In 1679 she published her first work
on the subject, *Der Raupen wunderbare Verwandlung und*
sonderbare Blumennahrung (The caterpillar, marvelous transformation, and strange floral food).

The highlight of her investigations was an expedition
to study the tropical plant and animal world in Surinam,
which she undertook from 1699 to 1701 with her daughter
Dorothea. The rich yield and the discoveries made
on this journey are documented in her magnum opus,
Metamorphosis Insectorum Surinamensium, published
in Amsterdam in 1705.

Plate VII (left) shows a branch of American cherry with
a caterpillar and the butterfly that develops from it; Plate XI
(right) shows a native palisade tree with the metamorphosis
of a moth.

Johann Miller, *Illustratio systematis sexualis linnaei per Johannem Miller,* **London 1777. Classis XIX. Ordo I. Syngenesia Polygamia Aequalis. Leontodon. Dandelion**
Illustrated book with hand-colored etchings, 54.5 × 38 cm
Museum für Gestaltung Zürich, Grafiksammlung

....

Johann Wolfgang von Goethe, *Durchgewachsene Nelke* **(A Proliferous Carnation), n.d.**
Pencil drawing, 47 × 34 cm
From: *Die Metamorphose der Pflanzen (Metamorphosis of Plants),* 1790. Edition, Berlin: W. Junk, 1924, with the original illustrations, edited by Julius Schuster
Illustrated book, 33 × 26 cm
ETH-Bibliothek, Swiss Federal Institute of Technology (ETH), Zürich, CH

Johann Miller's illustrations, here of a dandelion, date back to *Systema Naturae* by Carl von Linné—published for the first time in 1735 and constantly expanded until the thirteenth edition in 1770—which revolutionized the systemization and classification of nature. The basis of his classification was the sexual system of plants with their male and female reproductive organs. In addition, Linné introduced binomial nomenclature. This two-part naming system, still in use today, designates first the genus and then the species both for plants as well as animals—Homo sapiens being the best-known example.

For Johann Wolfgang von Goethe, on whom Linné had a great influence, the pursuit of nature was just as important as that of literature and philosophy, and his scientific writings on botany, zoology, geology, and meteorology are correspondingly extensive. In his *Metamorphose der Pflanzen* he describes the successive growth and reproduction process of plants, and from it attempts to derive a basic theory. He expresses his concern in the elegy of the same name from 1798: "Thou art confused, my beloved, at seeing the thousandfold union / Shown in this flowery troop, over the garden dispers'd; [...] None resembleth another, yet all their forms have a likeness; / Therefore, a mystical law is by the chorus proclaim'd; / Yes, a sacred enigma! Oh, dearest friend, could I only / Happily teach thee the word, which may the mystery solve!"

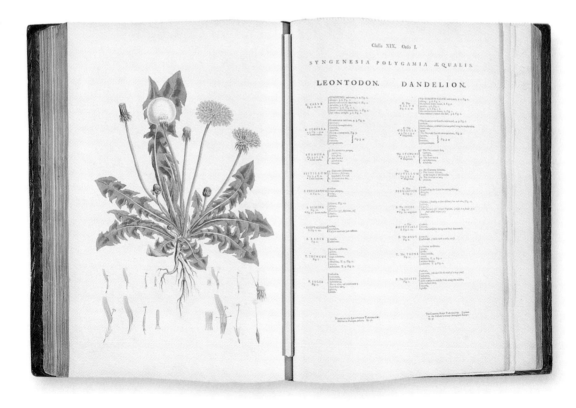

Marco Leonti with Herbario Nacional MEXU, *Plantas medicinales de los Populacas de la Sierra Santa Marta*, Veracruz, MX

Family: Crassulaceae, Latin name: Kalanchoe calycinum Salisb., found: Santa Rosa Loma Larga, Municipio of Hueyapan de Ocampo, in the garden of the Hospital of Traditional Medicine, used to treat fever, collected: 12/18/1999
and
Family: Cecropiaceae, Latin name: Cecropia obtusifolia Bertol., found: Soteapan, Municipio of Soteapan, used to treat diabetes, collected: 10 / 20 / 1999
Sheets with dried plants, each 43 × 27.5 cm
Institute of Pharmaceutical Sciences, Department of Applied Biosciences, Swiss Federal Institute of Technology (ETH), Zürich, CH. Institut für Systematische Botanik, Universität Zürich, CH.

....

Frank Shipley, Isaac Holden, William Albert Setchell, *Phycotheca Boreali-Americana – A collection of dried Specimens of the Algae of North America*, 2 vols., Malden, Massachusetts, 1899. XV. Ascophyllum nodosum (L.) Le Jolis. On Rocks in littoral zone, Bridgeport, Connecticut, May 1899, Isaac Holden. ♀ a With oogonia, ♂ b With antheridia
Book with dried algae
Institut für Systematische Botanik, Universität Zürich, CH

Johannes Gessner, *Hortus Siccus*, ca. 1783.
Achillea macrophylla
Bound herbarium, 50 × 35 × 15 cm
Institut für Systematische Botanik, Universität Zürich, CH

Plantas medicinales de los Populacas de la Sierra Santa Marta, Veracruz, Mexico.

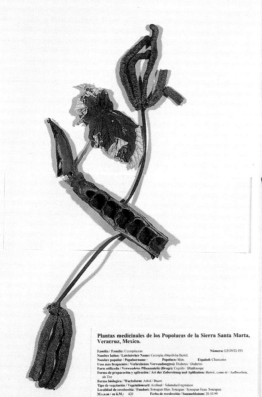

Plantas medicinales de los Populacas de la Sierra Santa Marta, Veracruz, Mexico.

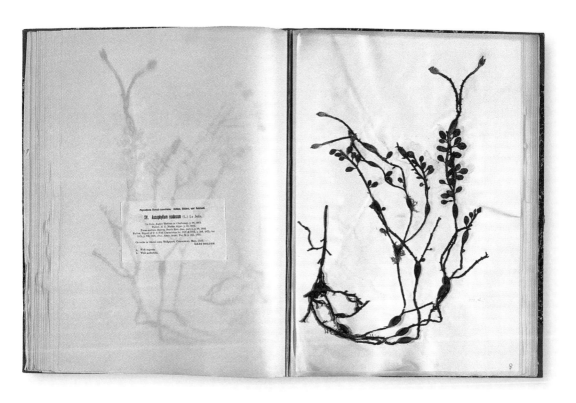

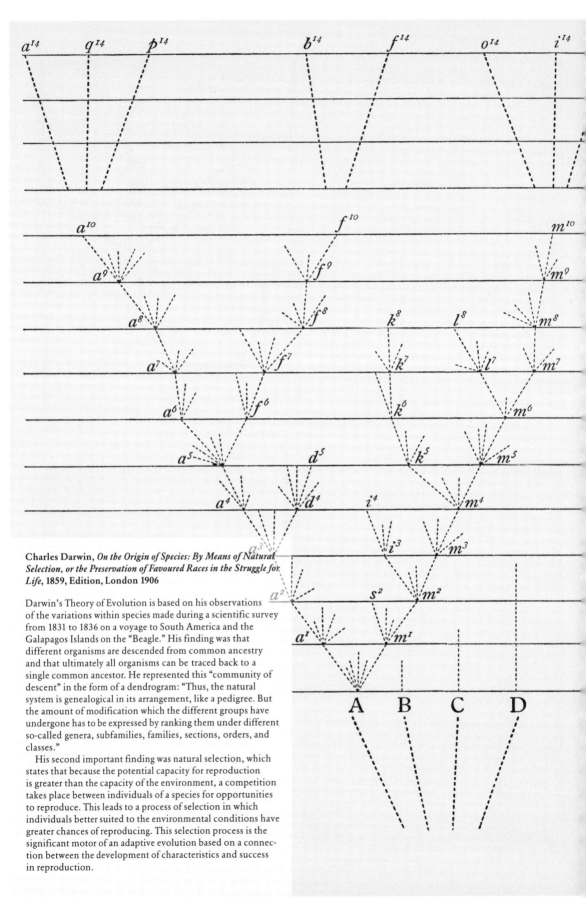

a^{14} q^{14} p^{14} b^{14} f^{14} o^{14} i^{14}

a^{10} f^{10} m^{10}

a^9 f^9 m^9

a^8 f^8 k^8 l^8 m^8

a^7 f^7 k^7 l^7 m^7

a^6 f^6 k^6 m^6

a^5 d^5 k^5 m^5

a^4 d^4 i^4 m^4

a^3 i^3 m^3

a^2 s^2 m^2

a^1 m^1

A B C D

Charles Darwin, *On the Origin of Species: By Means of Natural Selection, or the Preservation of Favoured Races in the Struggle for Life*, 1859, Edition, London 1906

Darwin's Theory of Evolution is based on his observations of the variations within species made during a scientific survey from 1831 to 1836 on a voyage to South America and the Galapagos Islands on the "Beagle." His finding was that different organisms are descended from common ancestry and that ultimately all organisms can be traced back to a single common ancestor. He represented this "community of descent" in the form of a dendrogram: "Thus, the natural system is genealogical in its arrangement, like a pedigree. But the amount of modification which the different groups have undergone has to be expressed by ranking them under different so-called genera, subfamilies, families, sections, orders, and classes."

His second important finding was natural selection, which states that because the potential capacity for reproduction is greater than the capacity of the environment, a competition takes place between individuals of a species for opportunities to reproduce. This leads to a process of selection in which individuals better suited to the environmental conditions have greater chances of reproducing. This selection process is the significant motor of an adaptive evolution based on a connection between the development of characteristics and success in reproduction.

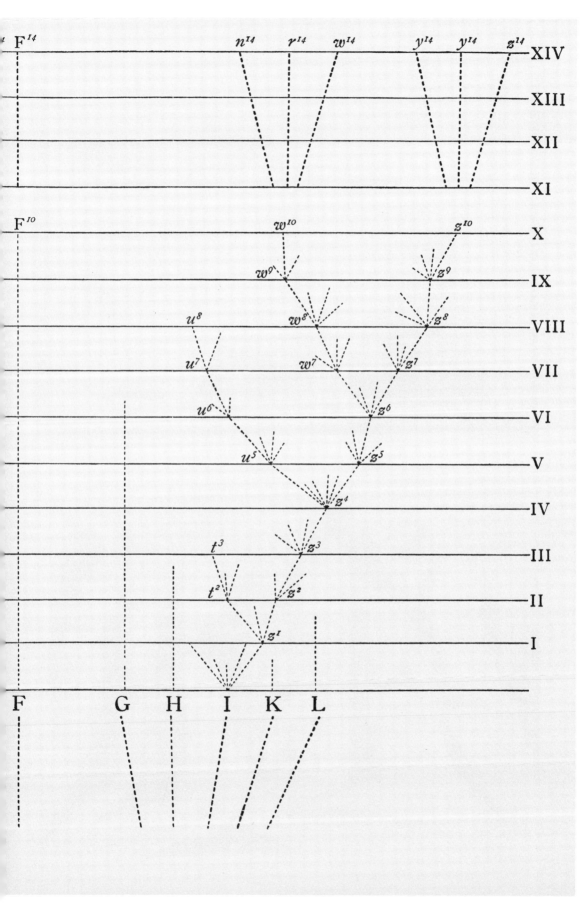

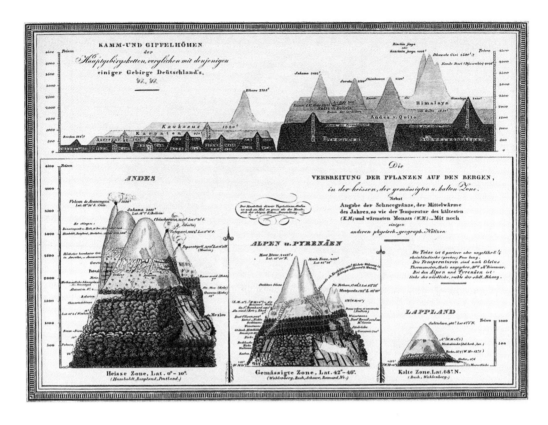

Heinrich Berghaus, *Physikalischer Schul-Atlas*
(Physical Atlas), Gotha 1850. Plate No. 20, "Ridge
and Peak Heights…"
Copper engraving, hand-colored, 40 × 30 cm
Reproduction from: Reprint, *Dr. Heinrich Berghaus' Atlas zum
"Kosmos" von Alexander von Humboldt*, Braunschweig n.d.
Private Collection
....

Johannes Jacobus Scheuchzerus, *Itinera per Helvetiae
alpinas regiones facta …*, 2 vols., Petrus Vander, Leyden 1723
Illustrated books, each 25.5 × 21 cm
Museum für Gestaltung Zürich, Grafiksammlung

The work of the naturalist Alexander von Humboldt is also
based on expeditions, particularly his American expedition
(1799–1804) and his Russian expedition (1829), combined
with scientific fieldwork in the fields of physics, chemistry,
geology, mineralogy, volcanology, botany, zoology,
climatology, oceanography, and astronomy. "What bestowed
upon me the main driving force was the endeavor to understand the phenomena of physical things in their general
relations, and nature as a whole, moved and vitalized through
inner powers," wrote the polymath in his magnum opus
published between 1845 and 1862, *Kosmos. Entwurf einer
physischen Weltbeschreibung (Cosmos: A Sketch of the Physical
Description of the Universe)*, which represents a summary
of his life's scientific achievement.

What distinguishes Humboldt is not only his findings
based on empirical research—he is among other things the
founder of plant geography—but also his transdisciplinary
scientific thought.

Page 24/25
For the biologist Ernst Haeckel, steeped in the tradition of
eighteenth-century natural history and an exponent of
Charles Darwin's theory of evolution, "the observation of
nature itself was the highest form of knowledge of nature."
His discoveries of marine single-cell organisms, which
in 1862 he brought together into artistic compositions in
his *Radiolarien-Atlas* and in 1899–1904 in *Kunstformen der
Natur*, are systematic representations which show the
process of evolution and, at the same time, an aesthetization
of nature in which nature becomes ornament.

Haeckel's influence, particularly on Art Nouveau,
is significant, and can be seen in the works of Hermann
Obrist, August Endell (see pages 90–93), Joseph Maria
Olbrich, and Louis Comfort Tiffany among others. René
Binet also took inspiration from Haeckel's illustrations
(see page 57), not only in his *Esquisses décoratives* published
in 1902, but also in his design for the monumental entrance
gate to the 1900 Paris World's Fair "in the interest of architecture or of ornament."

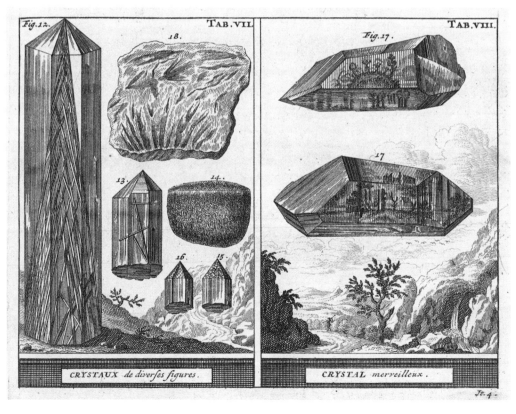

Ernst Haeckel, *Discomedusae – Scheibenquallen* **(Scyphozoa)**
From: *Kunstformen der Natur*, plate 28, Leipzig 1897–1904
Lithograph, 36×27.5 cm
Museum für Gestaltung Zürich, Grafiksammlung

Ernst Haeckel, *Platodes – Plattentiere* **(Flatworms)**
From: *Kunstformen der Natur*, plate 75, Leipzig 1897–1904
Lithograph, 36 × 27.5 cm
Museum für Gestaltung Zürich, Grafiksammlung

Model of cell division, ca. 1900
Wax on wooden bases, each 13 × 7 cm
Universität Zürich, Zoologisches Institut, Prof. Dr. Blanckenhorn

Zoological preparations. Nymphalidae
Details from specimen case, 50.5 × 42 × 7 cm
Universität Zürich, Zoologisches Institut, Prof. Dr. Blanckenhorn

Plant models, ca. 1900
Painted wood, up to 47 × 16 cm
B. Brendell, Berlin. Institut für Systematische Botanik,
Universität Zürich, CH

1

2

4

3

John Ruskin, *The Stones of Venice*,
1851–53. Vol. II, *The Sea-Stories*, with
illustrations by the author. New
edition in small form, Sunnyside:
Orpington: George Allen, 1898.
Illustration 23, *The Acanthus of Torcello*
Illustrated book, 19.5 × 14 cm
ETH-Bibliothek, Swiss Federal Institute
of Technology (ETH), Zürich, CH

5

J. Ruskin

J.H. Le Keux

John Allen

23. The Acanthus of Torcello.

Eugène Emmanuel Viollet-le-Duc,
Dictionnaire Raisonné de l'Architecture
Française, du XIe au XVIe siècle,
Paris: A. Morel Editeur, 1867. Vol. 2,
Balustrade, fig. 10, page 77 (balustrade
executed from 1230 to 1240)
Illustrated book, 23.5 × 17 cm
ETH-Baubibliothek, Swiss Federal Institute
of Technology (ETH), Zürich, CH

Both John Ruskin's drawing of an
acanthus cap with its models in nature,
and Eugène Emmanuel Viollet-le-Duc's
depiction of the detail of a balustrade,
show the nineteenth-century interest in
the use of natural forms in architecture.

Eugène Samuel Grasset, *Pflanzen- und Landschaftsstudien*
(Plant and landscape studies), 1890–1903
Pencil drawings, 36.5 × 25.5 cm
Museum für Gestaltung Zürich, Grafiksammlung

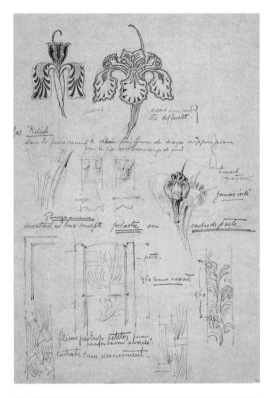

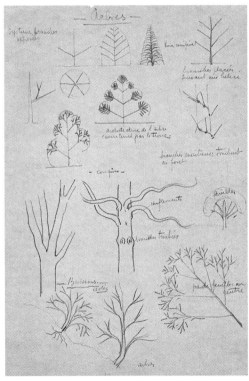

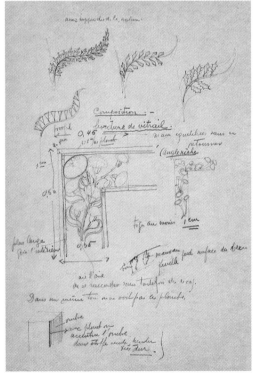

traduction.

formes

*On pourrait
aussi tenir
compte de la
perspective.*

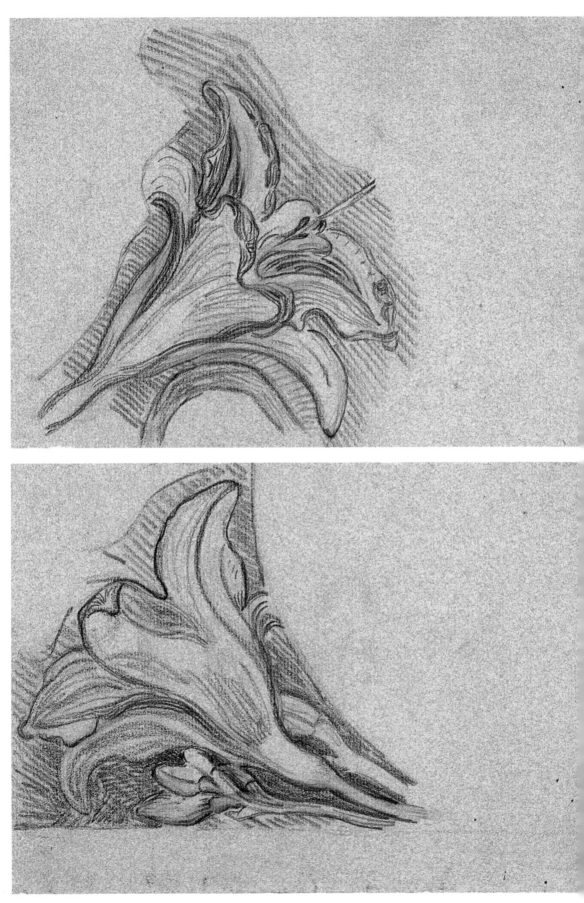

Henry van de Velde, *Studien zu Lilienblüten*
(Studies of lily flowers), n.d.
Conté crayon on rough gray paper, 31.5 × 24 cm
Museum für Gestaltung Zürich. Grafiksammlung

Henry van de Velde, *Sonnenblumen. Studie mit stark*
ornamentalisierten und stilisierten Sonnenblumen
(Sunflowers: Study with heavily ornamentalized
and stylized sunflowers), n.d.
Charcoal on rough gray paper, 24 × 31.7 cm
Museum für Gestaltung Zürich. Grafiksammlung

The transition from the study of nature to design
approaches inspired by nature can be seen in the drawings
of Eugène Grasset and Henry van de Velde.

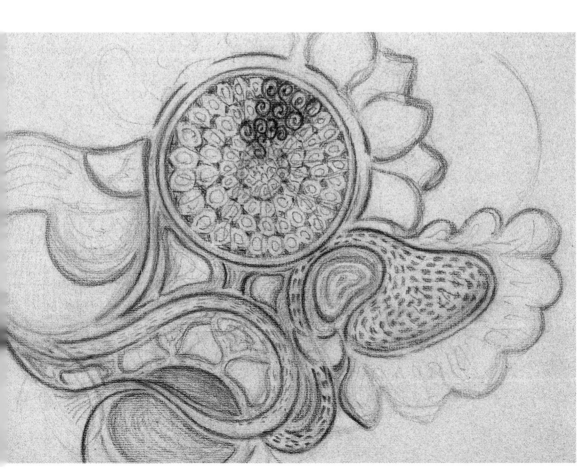

Karl Blossfeldt, Bronze models, so-called Meurer Bronzes.
Knospe vom Ahorn, Sambucusknospe geschlossen,
Laubknospe vom Sambucus, Knospe der Campanada
Medium (Maple bud, closed elder bud, elder foliage bud,
Campanada Medium bud), n.d.
Bronze models, with base: 26.5 cm, 23.5 cm, 30.5 cm, 29.5 cm
Universität der Künste, Universitätsarchiv, Berlin, DE

Karl Blossfeldt, Bronze models, so-called Meurer Bronzes.
Füllblatt der Distelblüte gross, Distelblatt (Petal of the
thistle flower, large, thistle leaf), n.d.
Bronze models, with base: 29.5 cm, 39 cm
Universität der Künste, Universitätsarchiv, Berlin, DE

"The plant should be appraised as a thoroughly artistic-architectonic structure. Besides an ornamental-rhythmic, creative primal drive, which prevails everywhere in Nature, the plant only constructs useful and purposeful forms. … It constructs according to the same laws which every master builder must also respect. But the plant never degenerates merely into the form of sober practicality, it shapes and models according to logic and usefulness and with primal force compels everything towards the highest artistic form." (Karl Blossfeldt in the preface to *Wundergarten der Natur*, Berlin 1932)

Karl Blossfeldt is known principally for the photographs he published in 1928 in *Urformen der Kunst,* and in 1932 in *Wundergarten der Natur,* and he is one of the most important representatives of Neue Sachlichkeit (New Objectivity).

Later reception mostly views the works independently of their origins—conceived originally as educational aids. Blossfeldt taught modeling of living plants at the Kunstgewerbeschule (School of Applied Arts) in Berlin, and for this purpose created a comprehensive work comprised of photographs, sculptures, and herbaria. The abstract and tectonically-accented sculptures of plants, the so-called Meurer Bronzes, were produced for the research and lessons of his own teacher Moritz Meurer, most likely at the end of the nineteenth century, and are thereby placed in the context of the contemporary study of nature along with Ernst Haeckel and Gottfried Semper's search for a new style. Meurer regarded the sculptures more as inspiration than as direct models. With their help, the decorative, flat ornamentation of Historicism was to be overcome.

Bruno Taut, Franz Hoffmann, Glashaus (Glass Pavilion) at the exhibition of the Deutscher Werkbund (German Work Federation), Cologne 1914
Exterior view
Photograph
Akademie der Künste, Berlin, DE, Bruno Taut-Archiv

Bruno Taut, Franz Hoffmann, Glashaus at the exhibition of the Deutscher Werkbund (German Work Federation), Cologne 1914
Interior view
Photograph
Akademie der Künste, Berlin, DE, Bruno Taut-Archiv

In the correspondence of the avant-garde architecture circle the Gläserne Kette (Glass chain) in 1920, Angkor (pseudonym of Hans Luckhardt) describes the basic principles for the use of natural forms, which also apply to the creative process: "What is essential is that the forms should not be replicated from nature as landscape, but must be of the same essence. Architecture should not imitate nature but must be nature itself." In accordance with this, Bruno Taut's Glashaus from 1914—dedicated to Paul Scheerbart and his *Glasarchitektur* (Glass architecture)—and Hans Scharoun's drawings and watercolors in the environment of the Gläserne Kette, no longer represent nature as ornament but as organism: in forms of growth, of sprouting up and budding in various stages of development from seed to fully open flower.

In his *Alpine Architektur (Alpine Architecture)*, published in 1919/20, Bruno Taut builds over his selected natural formations, the "organs of the godhead Earth" with glass structures that take up again the style of the Glashaus. The utopian work produced under the impression of the First World War was intended to unite mankind in a great task, which from the "crystal building" progresses via the "architecture of mountains," the "Alpine building" to the "earth crust building," and finally to the "star building," which ends in the "great nothingness" written in the form of an egg.

7

Bruno Taut, *Alpine Architektur*
(Alpine Architecture), 1919/20
Der Kristallberg (The Crystal Mountain), 2nd Part: Architektur
der Berge (Architecture of the Mountains), Sheet 7
Pen in gray and black, brush in gray, pencil sktech, on paper,
49.6 × 50 cm
Akademie der Künste, Berlin, DE, Archiv Baukunst

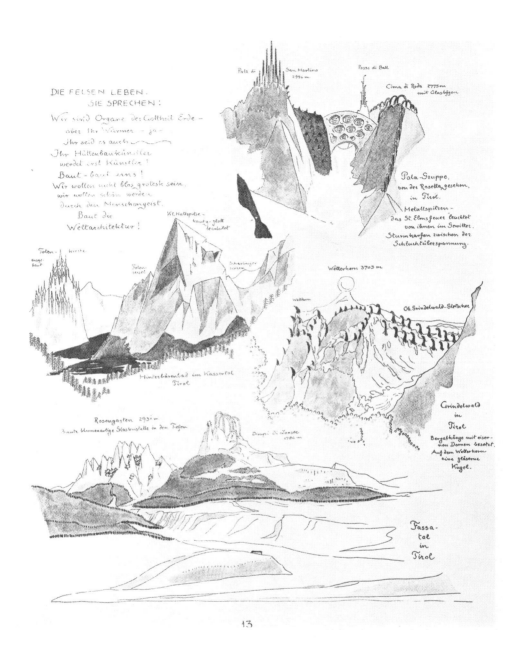

DIE FELSEN LEBEN.
   SIE SPRECHEN:

Wir sind Organe der Gottheit Erde –
   aber Ihr Würmer – ja –
   Ihr seid es auch.
Ihr Hüttenbaukünstler
   werdet erst Künstler!
Baut – baut uns!
Wir wollen nicht blos grotesk sein,
   wir wollen schön werden
   durch den Menschengeist.
   Baut die
   Weltarchitektur!

Pala di
San Martino
2996 m

Passo di Ball

Cima di Roda 2775 m
mit Glasbögen

Pala-Gruppe,
von der Rosetta gesehen,
in Tirol.
Metallspitzen –
das St. Elmsfeuer leuchtet
von ihnen im Gewitter.
Sturmharfen zwischen der
Schluchtüberspannung.

Kl. Halbspitze –
Kante glatt
beleuchtet

Schneiger
Schrein

Toten-
kirche
ausge-
baut

Toten-
insel

Wetterhorn 3703 m

Wetterhorn

Ob. Grindelwald-Gletschee

Hinterbärenbad im Kaisertal
Tirol

Rosengarten 2951 m
Bunte blumenartige Glaskristalle in den Tiefen

Dirupi di Larsec
2786 m

Grindelwald
in
Tirol
Bergabhänge mit eiser-
nen Domen besetzt.
Auf dem Wetterhorn
eine gläserne
Kugel.

Fassa-
tal
in
Tirol

13

Bruno Taut, *Alpine Architektur*
(Alpine Architecture), 1919/20
Felsgegenden in Tirol (Rocky Areas in Tyrol), 3rd Part:
Der Alpenbau (The Alpine Building), Sheet 13
Pen and brush in black and gray, pencil sketch, on paper,
56.2 × 76.5 cm
Akademie der Künste, Berlin, DE, Archiv Baukunst

Hans Scharoun, *Volkshausgedanke*
(Volkshaus Thought), 1920
Pen and India ink on paper, 26.5 × 21.4 cm
Akademie der Künste, Berlin, DE, Archiv Baukunst

Hans Scharoun, *Stadtwerden*
(Becoming City), 1919–21
Watercolor, 37.8 × 27.6 cm
Akademie der Künste, Berlin, DE, Archiv Baukunst

NATURE'S ARCHITECTURE: THE QUEST FOR THE LAWS OF FORM AND THE CRITIQUE OF HISTORICISM

Barry Bergdoll

The explosion of natural forms in the vocabulary of Jugendstil has long seemed a radical rejection of the historicist ethos which reigned throughout the nineteenth century. Yet the conviction that research into the underlying form-giving mechanisms of nature could provide creative impulses in design had been a leitmotif of architectural thought for well over a century when, in the 1890s, Victor Horta and Henry van de Velde in Brussels; Hector Guimard, René Binet, and others in Paris; Antoni Gaudí in Barcelona; Hermann Obrist and August Endell in Munich; and Louis Sullivan in Chicago, among so many others, turned to forms resonant with natural laws of growth to guide their quests for a vocabulary freed from the imitation of historic styles. New standards in the observation and classification of the natural world initiated by Georges Buffon's *Histoire Naturelle* (1749–78) crested in the great wave of natural history museums created in the wake of the French Revolution's transformation of the Parisian Jardin du Roi into the public Muséum d'Histoire naturelle. The idea that the study of the generative laws underlying the diversity of natural form might engender an art which could itself parallel the productive forces of nature was a recurrent concern of architects and design theorists convinced of the adage, first explored by Goethe and other German Romantic theorists, that nature is characterized by underlying unity in variety.[1] Goethe thus transformed into a compelling research program a question first raised as early as 1757, when Moses Mendelssohn asked what natural and artistic beauty had in common. This fundamental challenge to idealist notions of imitation as the end of art in favor of a search for shared laws of development and formal generation was the very stuff of the new "science" Goethe labeled morphology, which became the framework from which his famous quest for the primordial plant developed.

Goethe's investigations would have little direct impact on architecture for more than a generation, not until, it would seem, they were popularized by his disciple and friend Alexander von Humboldt with his *Cosmos* lectures in Berlin (1827–28). These were delivered in the neoclassical Singakademie, a building for which Karl Friedrich Schinkel had drawn up the initial plans. In 1828, Schinkel helped Humboldt decorate the interior of Berlin's Schauspielhaus—with a décor evocative of his own 1816 stage designs for Mozart's Masonic *Magic Flute*—to receive the first convention of natural scientists (fig. 1). This close collaboration between natural scientist and architect developed into a sustained exchange of ideas, and Schinkel launched himself on a last great series of challenging stylistic experiments. His late brick works have generally been interpreted as a functionalist turn, but the project for a bazaar on Unter den Linden, the Packhof buildings along the Spree canal, the Bauakademie, as well as the unrealized design for the royal library, are also designs in which a search for the primordial forms of architecture brought the quest for the new into close dialogue with the romantic tradition of morphology. Here Schinkel pursued a radical reduction of the literal classical rendering of forms as well as links between the diverse styles that architecture had known historically, something commemorated most clearly in the sketch of the transformative process of the morphemes of construction from the earliest post and lintel spans and the earliest corbelled arches to all elaborated forms of these primordial motifs, a research project given compelling form in the incomplete didactic panorama of the so-called *Lange Blatt* (fig. 2).

Thirty-five years later, Friedrich Adler celebrated the Bauakademie as both a revival of Goethe's idea of the primordial seed and as an impetus for a new generation of natural historical and architectural research: "It was and still is a great original work. It belongs neither exclusively to antiquity, nor even less to the Middle Ages or to the Renaissance. It reveals the transcendence of any narrow historical attachment; it is like a grain of seed, which promotes further organic unfolding."[2] For Schinkel, the Bauakademie's meaning resided as much in its terra-cotta ornamentation as in its brick construction: "One must not understand the word ornament or decoration to signify the imitation of something that lies outside the object and its essence or essential idea."[3] "The window ledges represent various moments in the history of the development of

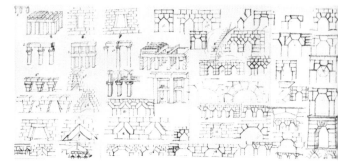

1 Karl Friedrich Schinkel, *Décor for the Meeting of Natural Scientists in the Schauspielhaus Berlin*, 1828.
Copper engraving, opaque color, 43.4 × 38.2 cm
Staatliche Museen zu Berlin, Kupferstichkabinett
2 Karl Friedrich Schinkel, Sketch for a Historical-Tectonic Introductory Course,
the so-called *Lange Blatt*, ca. 1823
Pen and pencil, 33.5 × 149.3 cm
Staatliche Museen zu Berlin, Kupferstichkabinett

the art of building, some examples of various periods and scenes representing the various types of work involved in building."[4] These are not elements of a stylistic chronology so much as they are the stages in the unfolding and development of a limited set of forms, a distinct parallel to Goethe's notion of the stages of development in crystals or plants. Just as the building itself synthesizes classical order and medieval vaulted construction, so architecture in all its diversity is portrayed as the product of a dialectic between the human search for order and the physical laws of tectonics. In the door frames, the human and natural histories of architecture are interwoven; the portal of the school represents architecture as fine art, while the portal to the architectural administration depicts architecture as science and technique. A parallel history of nature appears in the lowest panels, where a burst of leaves with thistles begins the organic theme continued on the reveal panels within the door portal (fig. 3). Here the plant forms do not repeat, as in conventional ornament, but sprout, grow, and flower. Paul Ortwin Rave first recognized that the plants were precisely those used by Goethe in *Metamorphosis of Plants* (1790) as the source for all morphological explanation and study.[5] In that book, which Schinkel received when he visited Goethe in Weimar in 1816, the poet explains that all previous natural history had concentrated on superficial taxonomies of form rather than on what he called the "inner economy" of organic form. He noted the

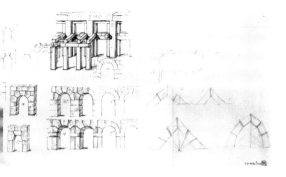

3 Karl Friedrich Schinkel, *Allgemeine Bauschule Berlin* (Building Academy),
main portal at the north facade, 1833. Pen, 52 × 42 cm
Schinkelmuseum, Berlin

morphological signs of development within each plant and explained the stages of plant development, which could reveal the generative and formal unity of the natural world. This primarily involved the study of the transformation of the leaf, which Goethe thought embodied the inner energy of the plant and thus its ability to generate its own characteristic forms from kernel to full blossom. This process he divided into six stages in three divisions. Schinkel's three principle registers correspond to the principle divisions of metamorphosis: seeding, growth, and propagation. In the law of transmutations, Goethe sought to demonstrate how "nature produces one part from another, and sets before us the most varied forms through the modification of a single order."[6] Morphology was all encompassing, at work in the form and transformation of all things, including minerals, clouds, animals, colors, and even human culture: "Just as the soul of nature has played itself out in the forms of its individual creations and the relationship of their parts one to another, so the human spirit has left its mark on the forms of art; from that a whole world of form has come into being."[7] Or in Schinkel's words: "Architecture is the continuation of nature in her constructive activity. This activity is conducted through that natural product: Mankind."[8]

Gottfried Semper, who referred to mankind as "der kleine Nachschöpfer"—the little re-creator[9]—was equally inspired by Humboldt, and by his insistence that the study of history and of nature were parallel quests for truth: "We find its noblest and most important result to be a knowledge of the chain of connections by which all natural forces are linked together, and made mutually dependent upon each other; and it is the perception of these relations that exalts our views and ennobles our enjoyments. [...] The unity which I seek to attain, the development of the great phenomenon of the universe, is analogous to that which historical composition is capable of acquiring."[10] Neither history nor nature could be studied independently, Humboldt insisted, for "in tracing the physical delineation of the globe we behold the present and the past reciprocally indicated, as it were with one another; for the domain of nature is like that of language, in which etymological research reveals a successive development by showing us the primary condition of an idiom reflected in the forms of speech of the present day."[11] Semper wrote to his publisher Vieweg in Braunschweig of Cuvier's displays, which had made such an impression on him in Paris that he was drawn to them "as if by a magical force": "Just as everything there envelops and is explained by the simplest prototypical form, just as nature in her infinite variety is yet simple and sparse in basic ideas, just as she renews continually the same skeletons by modifying them a thousand fold according to the formative stages reached by leaving beings and the conditions of existence [...] works of art are also based on certain standard forms conditioned by primordial ideas, yet permit an infinite variety of phenomena according to the particular needs that affect them."[12] By the late 1840s, Semper had drawn up a prospectus for a *Vergleichende Baulehre* (comparative building theory) modeled on Humboldt's *Cosmos*.

Semper, like Humboldt, was a go-between between the worlds of German and French natural science, just as he was a conduit for the great intellectual ferment of late French romanticism whose great moment of questioning coincided with the Cuvier-St. Hilaire debate, a debate Goethe took for a revolution more important than that which in July of the same year swept away the restored Bourbon monarchy and opened the era of the citizen-king Louis Philippe.[13] There is no single French text calling for a natural architecture or a natural history of architecture, but French romantic culture from Henri Labrouste to Eugène Emmanuel Viollet-le-Duc is riddled with references to then current scientific debates, as for instance Léonce Reynaud's famous quip, "One can, in a very profound way, compare human monuments with the shells formed by animals who leave there the imprint of their bodies even as they use them as their domicile; natural methods make no distinction between the description of the outer shell and the description of mollusks."[14] Goethe described a development that once progressed by stages and was radial in its development; form was generative, not static, yet the pattern was clear at any stage. Viollet-le-Duc's dictionary entry, "Style," is one of the century's most powerful statements of a monistic view of nature as underscored by fundamental geometric and spiritual unities. "Architecture as an art is a human creation. Such is our inferiority that, in order to achieve this type of creation, we are obliged to proceed as nature proceeds in the things she creates. We are obliged to employ the same elements and the same logical method as nature; we are obliged to observe the same transitions,"[15] he proclaimed.

Increasingly, architects' fascination with nature clung tenaciously to monism, with its unifying concepts, even in the face of the growing specialization of scientific research and the growing fragmentation of the natural order it depicted. With the exception of a few figures like Viollet-le-Duc, who undertook his own geological research in the Alps, and even proposed a monumental restoration of Mont Blanc, architects turned ever more frequently to popular science rather than to first-hand observation. Popular science proliferated in the press, such as the successful French *La Science pour tous,* or in the galleries of natural history museums, not least Paris's Muséum d'Histoire naturelle, whose great second phase of construction from the late 1860s coincides with a renewed episode in the discourse between the quest to penetrate to the underlying laws of form generation in nature and the quest for an architecture freed from antiquarian research. Just as the issue of new building types and new scales was presenting itself as one of the fundamental challenges to architects, so the number of new species was augmented, less by the conquest of new territories than through the application of more powerful forms of magnification, and by the rapid evolution of oceanography, seen by many as a glimpse not only into the depths of the unknown but also into the origins of the universe. Viollet-le-Duc already hints at this in the famous statement: "From the largest mountain down to the finest crystal, from the lichen to the oaks of our forests, from the polyp to human beings, everything in terrestrial creation does indeed possess style—that is to say, a perfect harmony between the results obtained and the means employed to achieve them."[16] (fig. 4)

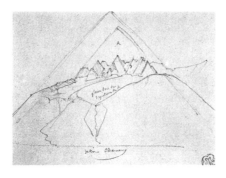

4 Eugène Emmanuel Viollet-le-Duc, *Chaîne des Aiguilles de Chamonix,*
reconstruction des états successifs, n.d.
Pencil, 16 × 21.4 cm
Fonds VlD

The architect Simon Claude Constant-Dufeux, today largely forgot-
ten, was in the mid-nineteenth century one of the most celebrated
teachers associated with both the École des Beaux-Arts and romanticism in architecture. He subscribed to the doctrine of Eclecticism defined by the philosopher Victor Cousin as a reaction against French
idealist aesthetics, particularly Cousins' axiom of "Unity in Diversity."
His leading pupil, Victor-Marie Ruprich-Robert, in turn, transformed
Constant-Dufeux's influential oral instruction into a published teach-
ing method (fig. 5). In July 1874, Louis Sullivan arrived in Paris from
Chicago, seeking from the outset a supplement to the formalism of the
École des Beaux-Arts, something, it would seem, that might resonate
with his own grounding in American transcendental philosophy. Rather
than turning, as many of the young students in the painting atelier did,
to popular sketching excursions to Fontainebleau, or even to the Jardin
des Plantes, Sullivan turned to the new school of ornamental research
centered around Ruprich-Robert. Sullivan's sketches after the plates of
Ruprich-Robert's great work *Flore ornementale* (1866–76), which contained a system of deriving ornament from an analytical study of plants,
often bear a dedication to John Edelmann, the young architect with
whom Sullivan had earlier spent time reading German natural philoso-
phers, including Goethe (fig. 6).[17]

Ruprich-Robert was one of several intermediaries between natural
science research and drawing instruction in mid-century Paris. Between
1855 and 1860, the German Karl Krumholz, returning from a three-year

 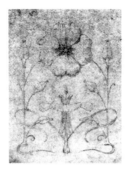

5 Victor-Marie-Charles Ruprich-Robert, *Flore ornementale*, Paris 1866–76, plate 108
6 Louis Sullivan, Tracing of plate 108 from Ruprich-Robert, *Flore ornementale*
Pencil on tracing paper, n.d.
The Art Institute of Chicago, Chicago

stay in England where he had been in the circles of design reformer Henry Cole and a group of artists also researching the application of botanical knowledge to design reform such as Owen Jones, Gottfried Semper, and Christopher Dresser, began work in Paris on his own illustrated works of plants, beginning with the publication of *Composition des fleures d'après nature... à l'usage des artistes industriels in 1859*. Krumholz's *Das vegetabile Ornament* of 1880, one of his last works, served in turn as a fundamental source for much of Jugendstil. Highly critical of the English theorist Owen Jones—whose famous *Grammar of Ornament* appeared in 1859—for reproducing ornament as historical information, and following a taxonomy of human civilization, Ruprich-Robert proposed instead that ornament could help designers escape from historicism. "It is all the more appropriate to have recourse to nature since our era is more than ever one of doubt, particularly in matters of art. If we see on the one hand some architects and artists, even with little encouragement, seeking a new way at the same time as most cannot seem to find anything better to do than to reproduce the artistic forms of those who have gone before, on the other hand there are new legions, learned to be sure, and captivated by the winds of industrial progress, who under the pretext of applying geometry to something useful end up expressing only dryness and impoverishment of form. [...] We seem to be unaware that above us reigns what we might call an amiably divine geometry which is also a geometry of utility, but at the same time a geometry of beauty, and whose elements are there in the very flowers which everyday we mindlessly trample upon."[18] Here in a nut-shell was that complex mixture of religious sentiment, almost pantheis-tic; of a belief that geometry was the link between divine intelligence and human imagination; and of a commitment to the world of nature as the matrix out of which Sullivan's complex and highly personal theory of ornament was to grow. Ruprich-Robert's plates are organized into three basic categories—leaves, buds, and flowers—before the stu-dent comes to the section on independent "compositions." Specimens are regularized, not to find a type but to create a normative model. No two leaves on a tree are identical, "and yet it is the same law which gave form to them, this very principle which I have sought to bring to light."[19]

For Sullivan, the French theorist's call for artistic freedom within the rules of nature's laws was, over the years, to become intertwined with his impassioned notions of American democracy and freedom; orna-ment, far from being an add-on, was at once to be an integral element of a rationalized structure, and at the same time a politic enabler. The impact of Charles Darwin's work echoes in Ruprich-Robert's call for freedom: "Indeed, there are types which have disappeared from the face of the planet, and there are others which we don't yet know, and noth-ing makes us believe that nature won't produce still others. The forms used by artists could well be the last [...] It really doesn't matter if the type that springs from his imagination already has its equivalent in nature as long as one finds no contradictions between its characteristics, and that one can see here unity and harmony, and that it is true from the viewpoint of the ideal [...] What would be an error in botany can-not be considered an error in the art of ornament."[20]

In Chicago, Sullivan worked towards developing an ornamental vocabulary that could harmonize with the then recent advances in engi-neering leading to the construction of new kinds of office buildings with metallic frames; he also began increasingly to draw the human figure and even to study musculature. By "organic," Sullivan—like his contemporary John W. Root—meant both that which related to the un-derlying orders of the natural realm and the old Aristotelian notion of an organism complete in and of itself. In 1906, in the essay "Ornament in Architecture," he summarized his philosophy: "The ornament [...] is applied in the sense of being cut in or cut on, or otherwise done: yet it should appear, when completed, as though by the outworking of some beneficent agency it had come forth from the very substance of the material and was there by the same right that a flower appears amid the leaves of its parent plant." [21] This sentiment remarkably parallels Schinkel of seventy years earlier, conceiving the skeletal forms and the floral ornament of the Bauakademie.

Sullivan's whole career might be summarized as the gradual realization of an ever-greater coordination of structure and ornament. "We feel intuitively that our strong, athletic, and simple forms will carry with natural ease the raiment of which we dream, and that our buildings thus clad in a garment of poetic imagery, half hid as it were in choice products of loom and mine, will appeal with redoubled power, like a sonorous melody overlaid with harmonious voices." [22] With the Wainwright Building (1891) in St. Louis, the ornament is subordinated to the muscular lines; with the Guaranty Building (1894) in Buffalo, every surface seems quite literally to leaf and to flower (fig. 7).

Sullivan's library is filled less with scientific treatises than it is with popular science. Most intriguing is the presence of one of the most influential scientists on the development of Jugendstil, the German biologist and oceanographer Ernst Haeckel who had traveled on the Challenger mission that in the 1870s charted the undersea world. Haeckel's work captivated a whole generation of artists—painters, decorative artists, and architects—with images of jellyfish, of coral, and of microscopic sea creatures, most notably radiolarian. While many scientists shunned Haeckel's work for its return to romantic science, artists reveled in the stunning images he provided in popular works, and latched on to Haeckel's commitment to a fundamental unity of natural form generation. The form in the seemingly amorphous, and the lack of a clear distinction between the animal and the vegetable realms, were among the subjects of Haeckel's research into the myriad of new species of microscopic life discovered in the sea, and transformed into the lurid color plates of his *Kunstformen der Natur* (1899–1904).

The impact of Haeckel's work on the Jugendstil imagination has been frequently discussed. August Endell's astounding façade of the Atelier Elvira in Munich (1896–97) seems to have been one of the first creations literally swept over in a tidal wave of enthusiasm for the splendors and mysteries that could emerge from even the basic laws of the simplest

7 Adler & Sullivan, Guaranty Building, Buffalo, New York, 1894–96
8 Ernst Haeckel, *Cyrtoidea. Flaschenstrahlinge*, plate 31 from *Kunstformen der Natur*,
Leipzig 1899–1904

of organisms. But perhaps no artist was more enamored with Haeckel's discoveries than René Binet, whose great metal portal to the Exposition Universelle of 1900 was nothing less than a monumentalized form of one of the phormocyrtida published by Haeckel in his 1887 *Report on the Radiolaria* (figs. 8 and 9).

Binet trained under Jules André, who had carried out the great mid-nineteenth-century expansion of the Muséum d'Histoire naturelle. The world of the miniscule and the previously invisible fascinated him, since with this explosion of new forms simple typologies of cellular structures were endlessly reproduced to create the most diverse forms responding to a whole ecology of functions and relations. The forty-five-meter-tall Porte monumentale was dwarfed by Eiffel's hundred-meter tower, with which it was polemically aligned, and to whose confidence in the reasoning of engineers he now juxtaposed the reasoning of nature.[23] The vast space beneath was created by a structure seated on only three substantial supports, brilliantly providing a dual axes to the fairground plan, but also pointing to Haeckel's admiration for nature as a rational designer that worked continually from geometric forms to find the strongest solution. Binet worked largely with a vocabulary of circles, spheres, and triangles to carry the strong flat cupola; more importantly, like the sponges and corals of Haeckel's universe, he conceived a form in which structure and decoration were integral, in which structure and space created one another.[24] For over a decade he maintained an active correspondence with Haeckel in Jena.

9 René Binet, *Porte Monumentale,* World's Fair, Paris, 1900
Friedrich-Schiller-Universität Jena, Institut für Geschichte der Medizin, Naturwissenschaft und Technik
«Ernst-Haeckel-Haus», Jena

In his *Esquisses décoratives,* a veritable lexicon of decorative designs,
Binet insists that these forms were not to be the basis of a new style.
Rather—in the sprit of Ruprich-Robert—his aim was to forge a philosophy of design in connection with the underlying laws of form generation in nature. In a dense series of introductory pages, dotted with
vignettes of the latest discoveries of the structural network of cell organization observed under the microscope, Binet urged architects to "turn
to the great laboratory of Nature, always in movement, always in production, without a moment of arrest or of hesitation."[25] The aim, Binet's
friend Gustave Geffroy explains, is not to create "Le Style Binet"—a coy
reference to Hector Guimard's marketing in those years of "Le Style
Guimard"—but rather to encourage readers to connect with Binet's
higher ambition: "The effort from which it derives will be retained,
categorized, and utilized by reason which embraces it for a whole order
of necessary works, and which will bring to the execution of those works
a remarkable spirit of unity and of method."[26]

The echo of Viollet-le-Duc could not be stronger. And in his fascination, shared by Haeckel, for the similarity of cells and crystals, Binet looks forward to one of the central fascinations of twentieth-century architecture—from the German Expressionists in the 1920s to the Metabolists in the 1960s—of finding a form of architectural abstraction in resonance with the building blocks of the universe.

1 Annika Waenerberg, *Urpflanze und Ornament: Pflanzenmorphologische Anregungen in der Kunsttheorie und Kunst von Goethe bis zum Jugendstil,* Commentationes Humanarum Litterarum 98, Helsinki, 1992.
2 Friedrich Adler, "De Bauschule zu Berlin von K. F. Schinkel" [1869], reprinted in *Schinkel zu Ehren: Festreden, 1846–1980,* ed. Julius Posener, Berlin, 1981, pp. 101–20. ["Sie ist und bleibt ein Originalwerk. Sie gehört nicht einseitig der Antike an, ebenso wenig dem Mittelalter als wie der Renaissance. Sie zeigt den engen geschichtlichten Anschluß frei überwunden; sie gleicht einen Samenkorn, das weitere organische Entfaltung entspricht."]
3 Karl Friedrich Schinkel, quoted in Goerd Peschken, ed., *Karl Friedrich Schinkel: Das Architektonische Lehrbuch,* Munich, 1979, p. 50.
4 K. F. Schinkel, *Sammlung Architektonische Entwürfe,* Berlin, 1819–40; reprint and translation in *Collection of Architectural Designs,* Chicago and New York, 1981, p. 49, pl. 118.
5 Paul Ortwin Rave, *Genius der Baukunst,* Berlin, 1944.
6 Johann Wolfgang von Goethe, *Metamorphosis of Plants,* sec. 3, trans. Agnes R. Arber in *Goethe's Botany: The Metamorphosis of Plants (1790) and Tobler's Ode to Nature (1782),* Waltham, Mass, 1946, p. 80. See also: Goethe, "The Morphology of Plants" and other natural history writings in *Goethe: The Collected Works; Scientific Studies,* ed. Douglas Miller, vol. 12, Princeton, 1988.
7 Ibid., p. 83. See also Barry Bergdoll, *Karl Friedrich Schinkel: An Architecture for Prussia,* New York, 1994, p. 208.
8 K. F. Schinkel, quoted in Peschken, *Das architektonische Lehrbuch,* p. 50.
9 Gottfried Semper, "On Architectural Styles" (1869) in *Gottfried Semper: The Four Elements of Architecture and other writings,* trans. Harry Francis Mallgrave and Wolfgang Hermann, New York, 1989, p. 268.
10 Alexander von Humboldt (probably paraphrasing the physiologist Carl Gustav Carus), in *Cosmos,* vol. 1, p. 41.
11 Ibid.
12 Gottfried Semper, "Prospectus, Comparative Theory of Building" (1852) in Mallgrave and Hermann, *Gottfried Semper: The Four Elements of Architecture,* p. 170.

13 Wolfgang von Goethe, "Réflexions sur les débats scientifiques de mars 1830 dans le sein de l'Académie des Sciences" in *Annales des sciences naturelles* 22 (1831): 179–93; reprinted in Goethe, *Gedenk-Ausgabe,* vol. 17, Zurich, 1952, pp. 380–414.
14 Léonce Reynaud, "Architecture" in *Encyclopédie nouvelle,* vol. 1, Paris, 1836, p. 777. ["On peut, dans un sens profond, comparer les monuments humains à ces coquilles formées par des animaux qui y mettent l'empreinte de leur corps et en font leur logis; les méthodes naturelles ne séparent point la description du test de la description des mollusques."]
15 E. E. Viollet-le-Duc, "Style", *Dictionnaire Raisonné de l'architectur...,* vol. 8, Paris, 1858–70, pp. 477–501. See English translation in Barry Bergdoll, ed., *Viollet-le-Duc: The Foundations of Architecture; Selections from the Dictionnaire raisonné,* introduction by B. Bergdoll, trans. Kenneth D. Whitehead, New York, 1990, p. 235. ["L'art de l'architecture est une création humaine; mais tels que soit notre infériorité, que pour obtenir cette création, nous sommes obligés de procéder comme la nature dans ses oeuvres, en employant … la même logique; en observant la même soumission à certaines lois…"]
16 Ibid. Translation from Bergdoll, ed., *Viollet-le-Duc: The Foundations of Architecture,* p. 240. ["Depuis la montagne jusqu'au cristal le plus menu, depuis le lichen jusqu'au chêne de nos forêts, depuis le polype jusqu'à l'homme, toute dans la nature terrestre, possède du style, c'est-à-dire l'harmonie parfaite entre le résultat et les moyens employés pour l'obtenir."]
17 David van Zanten, "Sullivan to 1890" in *Louis Sullivan: the function of ornament,* ed. Wim de Wit, New York, 1986, p. 34.
18 Victor Ruprich-Robert, *Flore ornementale: Essai sur la composition de l'ornement, éléments tires de la nature et principes de leur application,* Paris, 1876, p. 4. ["Il est d'autant plus à propos de recourir à la nature que notre époque est plus que jamais celle du doute, en fait d'art, et que si nous voyons, d'un côté, quelques architectes, quelques artistes trop peu encouragés, chercher une voie nouvelle lorsque d'autres ne trouvent rien de mieux à faire que de reproduire simplement les arts de ceux qui ne sont plus, il existe, de l'autre côté, de nouvelles légions, savantes il est vrai, écloses au souffle du progrès de l'industrie, et qui, sous prétexte

d'appliquer la géométrie de l'utile, n'expriment que sécheresse et pauvreté… On semble ignorer que règne au-dessus de nous tous ce que nous pourrions appeler la géométrie aimable de Dieu, géométrie qui est aussi celle de l'utile, mais en même temps celle de la beauté, et dont les éléments sont particulièrement dans les fleurs que chaque jour, sans y songer, nous foulons aux pieds."]

19 Ibid., p. 5. ["et cependant c'est une même loi qui les a formées. C'est cette loi, ce principe, que j'ai voulu faire ressortir."]

20 Ibid., p. 10. ["En effet, il est des types qui ont disparu de la surface du globe, il en est d'autre que l'on ne connaît pas encore, et rien ne nous assure que la nature n'en produira pas d'autres. Ceux que l'artiste conçoit peuvent encore être déjà de ceux-ci… Peu importe que le type sorti de son imagination ait sa réalisation dans la nature; pourvu qu'on n'y puisse saisir aucune contradiction entre les attributs, et qu'on y remarque l'unité et l'harmonie, il est vrai au point de vue de l'idéal… Ce qui serait une faute de bota-nique ne peut être considéré comme une faute dans l'art de l'ornement."]

21 Louis Sullivan, "Ornament in Architecture", *The Engineering Magazine* 3 (August 1892), p. 4.

22 Ibid., p. 1.

23 Binet's work has been the subject of much recent research and writing, see: Erika Krause, "L'influence de Ernst Haeckel sur l'Art Nouveau" in *L'âme au Corps: arts et sciences, 1793–1993,* ed. Jean Clair, Paris, 1993, pp. 242–51; Barry Bergdoll, "Les *Esquisses Décoratives de René Binet*" in *René Binet 1866–1911, un architecte de la Belle Epoque,* exh. cat., Musées de Sens, Sens, 2005, pp. 100–109; and most recently Robert Proctor, "Architecture from the cell-soul: René Binet and Ernst Haeckel", *The Journal of Architecture* 11, no. 4 (September 2006), pp. 407–24.

24 Recent research has shown possible contacts between Binet and Sullivan. See Marie-Laure Crosni-er-Lecomte, "René Binet" in *Thieme-Becker/Vollmer Gesamtregister: Register zum Allgemeine Lexikon der bildenden Künstler von der Antike bis zur Gegenwart und zum Allgemeinen Lexikon des XX. Jahrhunderts,* Munich and Leipzig, 1996.

25 Gustave Geffroy, preface to *Esquisses décoratives,* by René Binet, Paris, 1902–03, p. 1. ["s'adresser au grand laboratoire de la Nature, toujours en mouve-ment, toujours en production, sans un instant d'arrêt ni d'hésitation. Là, on peut obtenir le secret infaillible des créations et des transformations."]

26 Ibid. ["l'effort dont elle procède va se trouver fortement retenu, classé, et utilisé, par la raison qu'il embrasse pour tout un ordre de travaux nécessaires, et qu'il apporte à leur exécution un remarquable esprit d'unité et de méthode."]

SEA

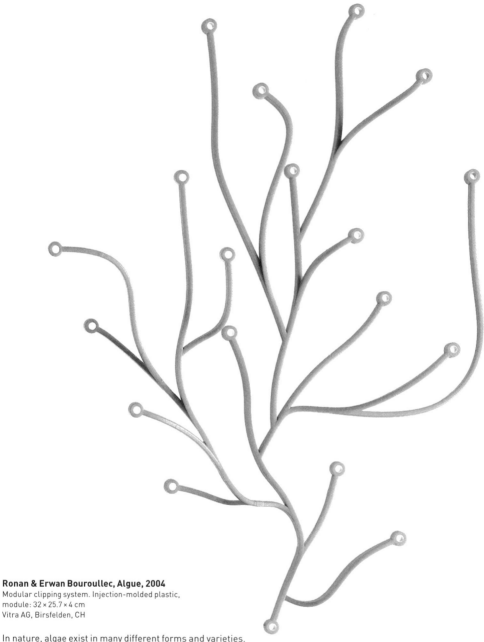

Ronan & Erwan Bouroullec, Algue, 2004
Modular clipping system. Injection-molded plastic,
module: 32 × 25.7 × 4 cm
Vitra AG, Birsfelden, CH

In nature, algae exist in many different forms and varieties.
They are generally the inhabitants of natural bodies of
water, where they contribute to the self-cleansing process,
but many have also adapted to living in the open air. The
latter certainly applies to the Bouroullec brothers' algae
modules that form their own finely branching ornament
which, thanks to thicker eyelet-like areas at the ends of
the module's total of nineteen points, can also be clipped
together at as many points as required to form complex
spatial meshes of different dimensions and thicknesses,
until an algae carpet is created.

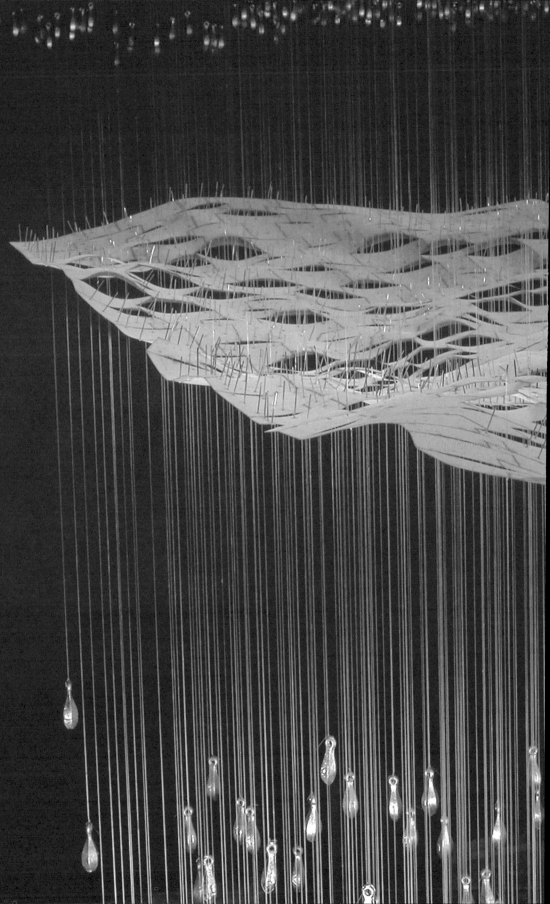

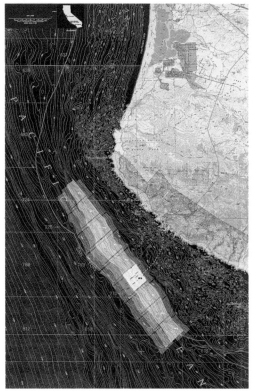

Yusuke Obuchi, Wave Garden, 2002
Installation. Styrene plastic film, monofilament,
122 × 183 cm, height variable
Yusuke Obuchi, London, GB

This innovative wave power station is a project for the
Californian coast designed to replace the nuclear energy
plant at San Luis Obispo. The floating, artificial landscape
made up of 1,734 small tile-like areas that, as a whole,
is roughly half as large as New York's Central Park,
would produce electricity from Monday to Friday by using
piezo-electronic sensors on the undersides of the surfaces
to transform the pressure of the Pacific's waves into
energy. On the weekend, when about 30 percent less
energy is required, a section of the elements rises above
the surface of the water to form an island that can be
reached by boat — the less energy required, the larger
the recreation landscape becomes. Wave Garden would not
only function as a producer but also as a visual indicator
of the varying amount of energy consumed, and therefore
would form an interface between the forces of nature
and the needs of society.

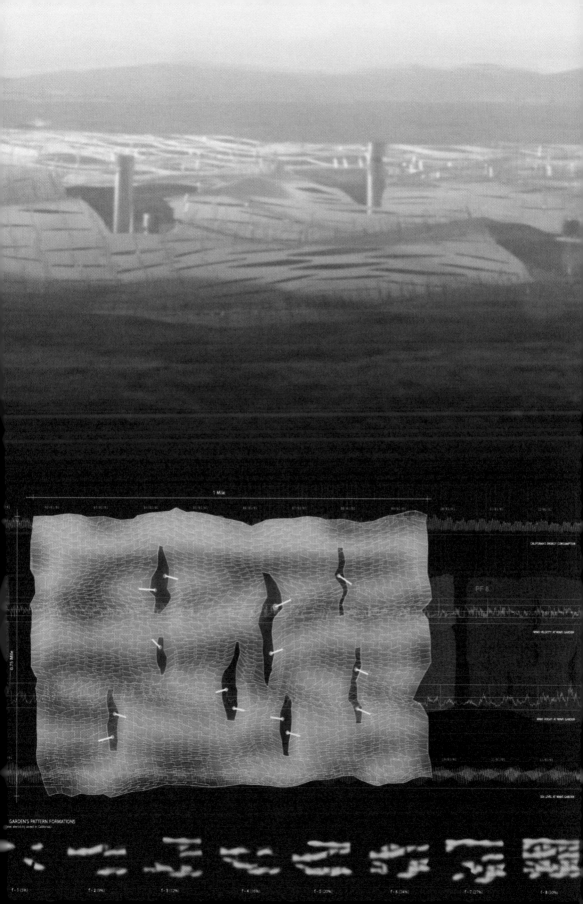

GARDEN'S PATTERN FORMATIONS
(over electricity saved in California)

Dale Chihuly, Shell, 1983
Shell with undulating walls in the form of a recumbent bivalve mussel in the
process of opening. Colorless glass with a blown, green cameo glass overlay.
Spun group of threads in dark red, colorless, and opaque pink; scattered
chips in yellow, orange, dark red, pink, turquoise, and light violet, melted on;
blown with eight-fold ribbed look, 16.2 × 30.5 × 20.4
Museum für Gestaltung Zürich, Kunstgewerbesammlung

Alvar Aalto, Savoy Vase, 1936
Mold-blown glass, coated, 16 × 20 × 17.5 cm
Iittala oy ab, Helsinki, FI. Museum für Gestaltung Zürich, Designsammlung

Ted Muehling, Coral Spoon, Salt/Pepper Snail, Moon Snail Bowl, Volute Bowl, 2000
Porcelain, lengths: 14 cm, 7 cm (each), 34 cm, 36 cm
Porzellan-Manufaktur Nymphenburg, Munich, DE

Marcel Wanders, Foam bowl, 1997
Porcelain, 17 × 3 cm
Moooi B.V., Breda, NL. Private Collection

Marcel Wanders, Sponge vase, 1997
Porcelain, 6 × 10 cm
Moooi B.V., Breda, NL. Museum für Gestaltung
Zürich, Designsammlung

Fernando and Humberto Campana, Anemone, 2001
Chair. Iron, 120 × 90 × 66 cm
edra Spa, Pisa, IT

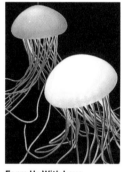

**Form Us With Love,
JellyFriends, 2005–07**
Lamp. Silicone, 50 × 40 × 40 cm
Form Us With Love,
Petrus Palmér, Kalmar, SE

**Michael Hübscher, Aquarium:
der Tausendundeinszweck-Halter, 1999**
Aquarium: The Thousand-and-One Uses Container.
Recyclable plastic, 12 × 20 × 20 cm
Hu:bschergestaltet, Michael Hübscher, Basel, CH

71

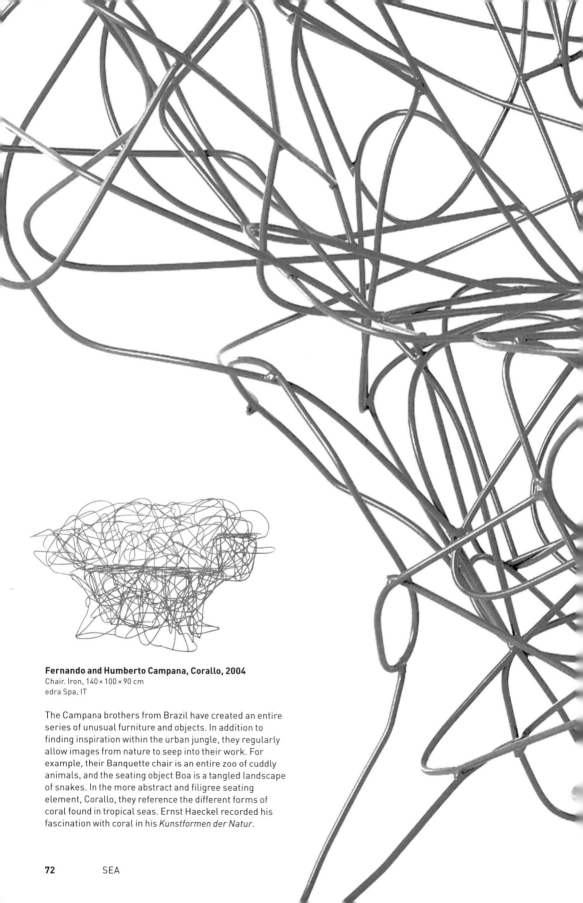

Fernando and Humberto Campana, Corallo, 2004
Chair. Iron, 140 × 100 × 90 cm
edra Spa, IT

The Campana brothers from Brazil have created an entire series of unusual furniture and objects. In addition to finding inspiration within the urban jungle, they regularly allow images from nature to seep into their work. For example, their Banquette chair is an entire zoo of cuddly animals, and the seating object Boa is a tangled landscape of snakes. In the more abstract and filigree seating element, Corallo, they reference the different forms of coral found in tropical seas. Ernst Haeckel recorded his fascination with coral in his *Kunstformen der Natur*.

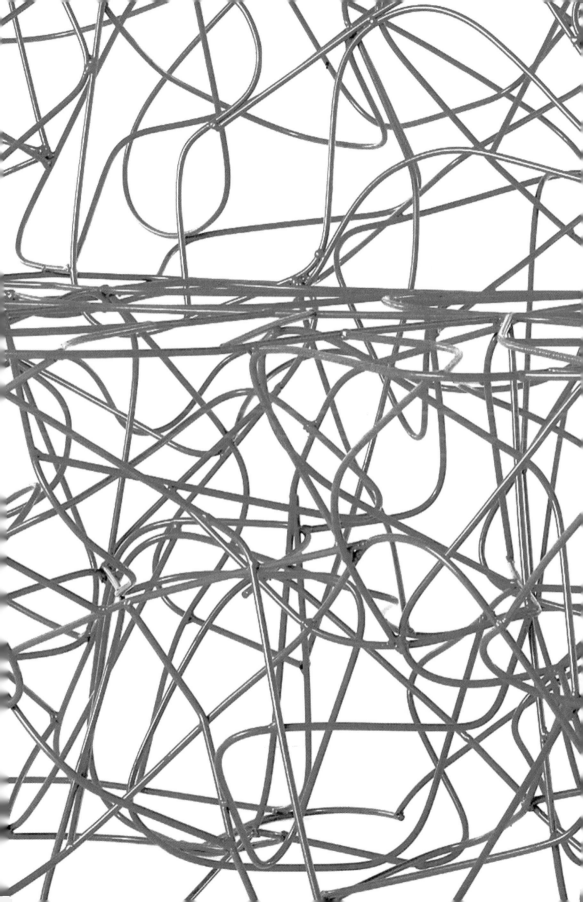

Speedo, Fastskin® FSII™ Bodyskin, 2004
High-tech swimsuit, full-body. 81 % Nylon / 19 % Lycra® spandex
Speedo, Reutlingen, DE. Sigi's Schwimmartikel, Wallisellen, CH

The research and development of these swimsuits for
competitive swimmers was based on the physiognomy of
the shark, in particular the nature of its skin and the way
the fish moves through water. The surface material of
the Fastskin® FSII is made up of different materials for
the different zones of the body, and thus mimics the small
panels of a shark's skin with their different degrees
of hardness that reduce frictional resistance and allow
optimal hydrodynamic efficiency. In combination with
body-scan technology and computer-aided water flow
analyses, this knowledge was applied to the athletes' bodies
and allowed the development of the fastest swimsuits
in the world. As with a diver's flippers, here too the fish
was the inspirational model for a successful development in the field of bionics.

Scubapro, Twin Speed, 2001
Fins. Thermoplastic: SEBS, Kraton, and EVA, each 68 × 25 × 10 cm
Tauchsport Turicum, Zurich, CH

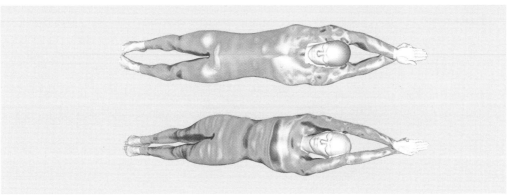

Werner Zemp + Partner Design, Trash Shark©, 2002
Chromium steel, polished natural colors, standard base of natural
chromium steel, dark grey powder-coated, 119.5 × 52 cm
Museum für Gestaltung Zürich, Designsammlung

Frank Gehry, Fish Bracelet, 2006
Wood and silver, 19.7 cm
The Frank O. Gehry™ Collection for Tiffany & Co.,
Tiffany and Company, New York, US

Frank Gehry, Pito, 1988
Kettle. Chromium-nickel steel,
solid mahogany, 23.5 × 21.2 × 18.2 cm
Alessi Spa, Crusinallo, IT. Museum
für Gestaltung Zürich, Designsammlung

Daimler Chrysler, Mercedes-Benz bionic car, 2005
Animation
DaimlerChrysler AG, Sindelfingen, DE

Bionics is a new research discipline in which the laws
of nature are harnessed for technological developments.
After a long period of research, the engineers of this
concept vehicle took as their model the tropical boxfish
with its angular and somewhat squat form. It has a stable
and light construction and ideal hydrodynamic qualities
that allow it to move its mass with a minimal expenditure
of energy. This vehicle, the first to be developed entirely
in accordance with the principles of bionics, is thus a
pioneer for a new generation of compact cars that have
minimal energy requirements and are consequently more
environmentally compatible.

ART NOUVEAU

There is probably no other era in which the influence of nature had such a fundamental importance as in the Art Nouveau period— not only by re-examining aspects of the Romantic thought represented by Johann Wolfgang von Goethe, which developed out of natural philosophy and traversed conventional categories; but also by offering itself as an alternative to industrialization and the mass production that came with it. Art Nouveau and its predecessor, the English Arts and Crafts movement, replaced the historicism of the nineteenth century.

Abandoning flat ornament, Art Nouveau predominantly employed motifs from the plant world as a structural element in design, transforming the object into an embodiment of life and the growth process inherent in its structure. These tendencies can be observed in both the floral as well as the more abstract versions of Art Nouveau.

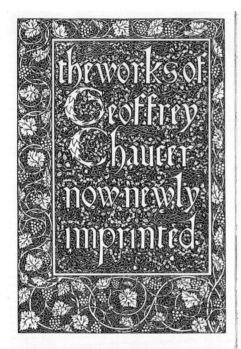

**William Morris, *The Works of Geoffrey Chaucer*, with illustrations
by Sir Edward Burne-Jones, Hammersmith: Kelmscott Press, 1896, GB**
87 woodcuts on handmade paper, exemplars on loose sheets, book size: 43 × 30 cm
Museum für Gestaltung Zürich, Grafiksammlung

Unknown, umbrella stand, before 1900
Cast iron, patinated. Floral reinterpretation of the object:
flower petals form the base, a stem with flower petals the shaft,
the irregularly-shaped opening a flower garland. The rococo-
like air shows French influence, 67 cm
Museum für Gestaltung Zürich, Kunstgewerbesammlung

**WMF, dish in the form of two water lily leaves,
held by a standing, winged figure, ca. 1900**
Tin alloy, molded, silver-plated, 21.1 × 29.1 × 23.2 cm
Museum für Gestaltung Zürich, Kunstgewerbesammlung

Henry van de Velde, candelabra, 1898/99
Cast brass, silver-plated. One of a pair.
Dynamic form, rigorously concentrated on the stem, with six
candle arms. In each case, three together as girandoles with
their height slightly offset against the other three, 58.5 cm
Bröhan-Museum. Landesmuseum für Jugendstil, Art Déco und
Funktionalismus (1889–1939), Berlin, DE

Two major directions in Art Nouveau are visible in these three silver objects: on the one hand, the floral direction with its plant ornamentation whose "long sensitive curves" reminded Nikolaus Pevsner of the stem of a lily, the feeler of an insect, the filaments of a flower, or sometimes a steeply shooting flame; on the other hand, the more abstract direction exemplified by Henry van de Velde, in which the ornamentation hardens into a more tightened line, passing into the structure of the object. These different tendencies, which partly interfuse, can also be observed in works of glass, ceramics, and furniture design.

**Emile Gallé, two-armed table lamp with
Chinese lanterns, ca. 1904**
Colorless glass with double overlay in salmon pink and dark red,
mold-blown. Decoration in simple raised etching, interior drawing
in flat, raised, and needle etching. Black lacquered iron mounting
with two intertwined stems with leaves, 51.7 × 30.9 × 24.9 cm
Museum für Gestaltung Zürich, Kunstgewerbesammlung

**Daum Frères, small bowl with deciduous woodland,
1903–05**
Colorless glass with yellow powder meltings, mold-blown.
Decoration in flat raised etching on rough matte base with brush-
applied enamels. In oblique view a foreshortened depiction
can be seen, 10.4 × 15.1 × 12.8 cm
Museum für Gestaltung Zürich, Kunstgewerbesammlung

**Emile Diffloth, Emile Decoueur,
and Taxile Doat, Gourd vases, ca. 1900**
Porcelain, 18.2 × 9.2, 24.2 × 8.8, 17.5 × 7 cm
Museum für Gestaltung Zürich, Kunstgewerbesammlung

Alfred William Finch, various vases, ca. 1904–07
Clay, matte glaze, ca. 20 cm
Museum für Gestaltung Zürich, Kunstgewerbesammlung

**Hermann Obrist, Wandbehang Alpenveilchen
(Cyclamen wall hanging), known as *Der Peitschenhieb*
(The Whiplash), signed "H", Munich 1894**
Base: silk, wool, cotton, lining: cotton, embroidery thread: silk,
technique: satin stitch, 120 × 184 cm
Münchner Stadtmuseum, Munich, DE

Der Peitschenhieb is not only one of the key works of
the Munich Jugendstil, but of the entire Art Nouveau
movement. The plant ornamentation becomes a
vibrant, sinuous line full of dynamism.

Carl Strathmann, *Angreifender Fisch*
(Attacking fish), ca. 1895
Watercolor and India ink drawing, 50.5×38 cm
Münchner Stadtmuseum, Munich, DE

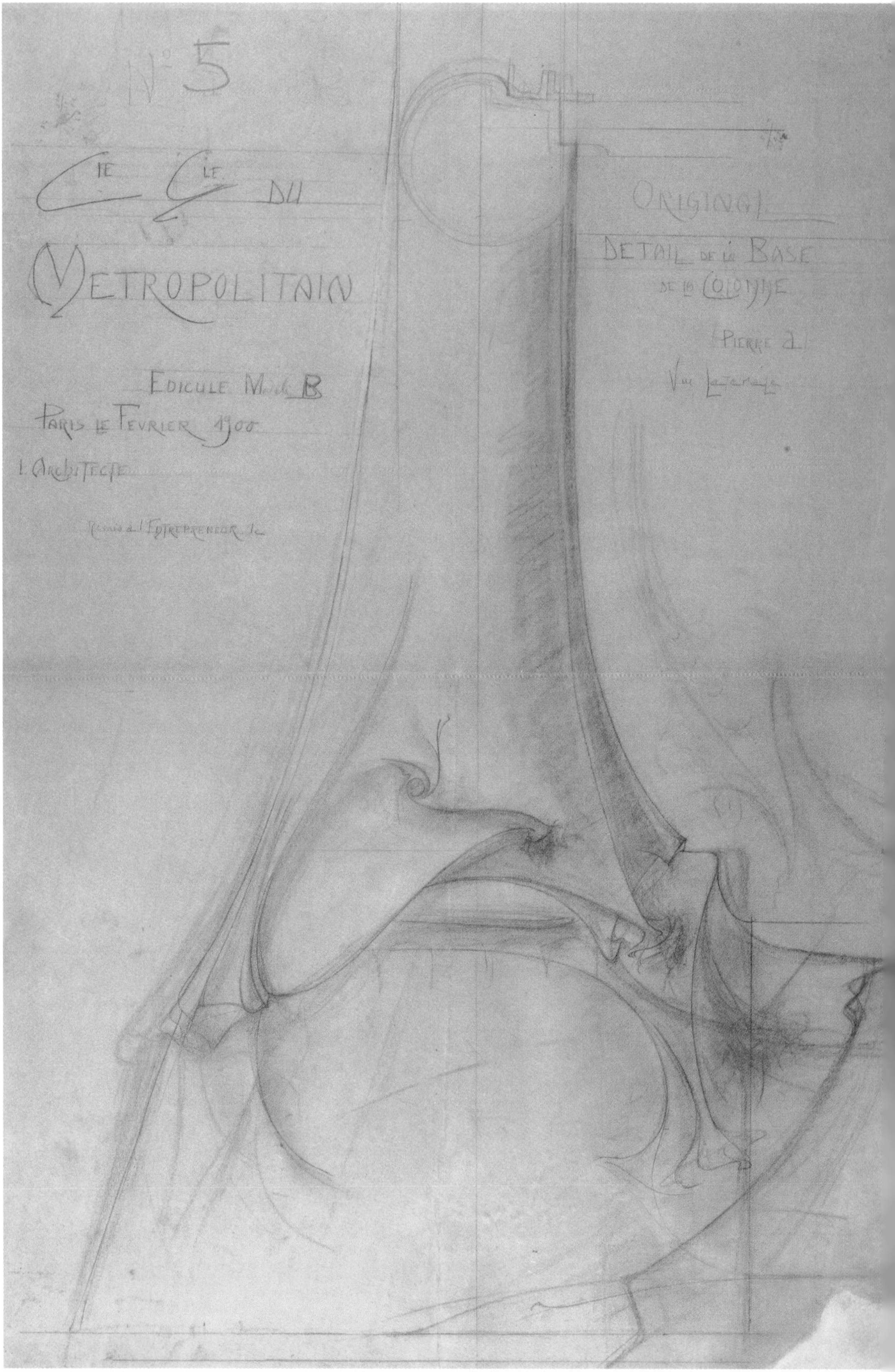

Nº 5

Cⁱᵉ Cⁱᵉ DU

METROPOLITAIN

ORIGINAL

DETAIL DE LA BASE
DE LA COLONNE

Edicule M. & B
PARIS LE FEVRIER 1900

L. ARCHITECTE

Pierre 2.

Vue Laterale

Remis a l'Entrepreneur Le

Hector Guimard, *Design for a column base*, ca. 1900.
Entrances and stairways of metro stations, Paris, 1899–1905
Drawing, 98 × 69 cm
Musée d'Orsay, Paris, FR

Hector Guimard, *Detail sketch for the balustrade*, 1900.
Entrances and stairways of metro stations, Paris, 1899–1905
Drawing, 74.5 × 140 cm
Musée d'Orsay, Paris, FR

The design of the entrances to the Paris Metro by
Hector Guimard around 1900 was an important public
commission that continues to characterize the city-
scape of Paris (see page 108). Guimard designed cast-iron
structures inspired by nature but not representing it.
Plant-like constructions, and the growth displayed in
them, can be seen in the slim, stem-shaped structures and
particularly in the preliminary sketches.

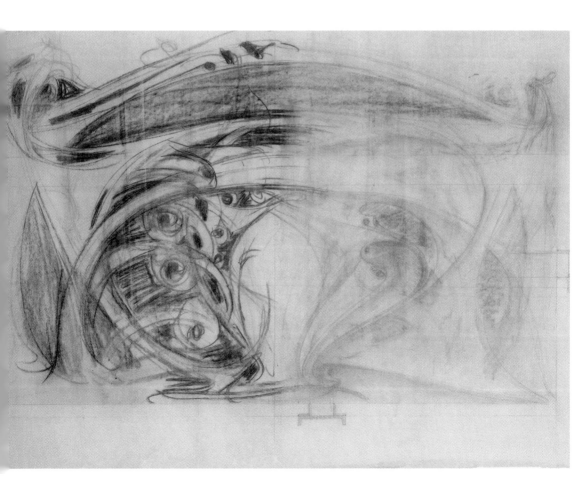

**Alphonse Maria Mucha, Monaco Monte Carlo –
Chemins de Fer P.L.M., 1897**
Lithograph, colored, 110.5 × 76.5 cm
Imprimerie F. Champenois, Paris, FR.
Museum für Gestaltung Zürich, Plakatsammlung

Alphonse Maria Mucha, JOB cigarette paper, 1896
Lithograph, colored, 66.5 × 46.5 cm
Imprimerie F. Champenois, Paris, FR.
Museum für Gestaltung Zürich, Plakatsammlung

ART NOUVEAU: THE SHAPE OF LIFE

Dario Gamboni

LIKE NATURE, NOT AFTER NATURE

A major tenet of German Romantic art theory was that the artist creates freely, and yet according to laws, like nature.[1] This idea located the law-abiding principle of art within the artist as analogous to and part of nature rather than in the exterior imitation of the products of nature, or in the observation of the man-made rules of academic doctrine and historic traditions. Like many aspects of Romantic thought, it was taken up in the late nineteenth century and formed a basis for what is variously called Art Nouveau, Liberty Style, Modern Style, Modernisme, or Jugendstil. Siegfried Bing declared nature to be "the infallible code of all laws of beauty," and the Swedish playwright and painter August Strindberg explained that the artist should "work like nature, not after nature."[2] Since Goethe's time, a technique had been devised to allow nature to depict itself: photography, which Henry Fox Talbot defined as "the pencil of nature." It is therefore not surprising that Strindberg experimented in the same years with photography in ways that connect it to the tradition of miraculous "acheiropoietic" images, images "not made by human hands": he regarded his *Celestographies* (fig. 1), the accidental result of plates dipped in developing fluid under the sky, as *vera icons* of the firmament.[3]

Strindberg, however, also resorted to slightly more orthodox ways of image making, such as oil painting, in which nature expressed itself as chance, spontaneity, or automatism.[4] Gauguin defined the artist as an extension of nature, an instrument of its continuing creation—an accomplice of *natura naturans* rather than a recorder of *natura naturata*.[5] Theories of agency can help us formulate more precisely what roles these conceptions assigned to nature, to the artist or designer,

1 August Strindberg, *Celestography*, 1894, photograph made without camera or lens
Royal Library, National Library of Sweden, Stockholm

and to the spectator or user of the works. The British anthropologist Alfred Gell has suggested a dialectical and extended notion of artistic agency, contending that not only the artist but the prototype (what the work represents), the "index" (the work itself), and the receiver (spectator or beholder) all are agents in the artistic process, and that conversely, depending upon the moment and the point of view, all are "patients."[6] In our case, we can say that the human creator was expected to delegate his or her agency to, or to derive it from, the active prototype nature. Or we can use the theory of economic agency and say that nature was seen as the principal and the human creator as its agent:[7] nature ordained and the artist executed, albeit with the crucial element of unpredictability inherent in such a relationship. As for the spectator/user, the artist as patient prefigured his or her position, and in turn he or she would be asked to appropriate the work in an active way, to become a part of the continuing process incorporated in it.

With notions such as *natura naturans* and automatism, we have located Art Nouveau in a historical (though somewhat sinuous) line stretching from the Renaissance to Surrealism through Romanticism and Symbolism. The forward-looking dimension of Art Nouveau, made manifest in its Surrealist reception, becomes clearer in its own time if one considers its relation to contemporary psychology.[8] For nature within oneself could also be called "the unconscious." In 1863, Théophile Gautier had described Victor Hugo's drawings as the result of "the chimeras of fantasy and [of] the fortuitous caprices of the unconscious hand."[9] In 1898, Odilon Redon defined his artistic process as a submission to *la fantaisie*, "the messenger of the 'unconscious,' that lordly and mysterious personage."[10]

TRUE TO THE MATERIALS

Redon also emphasized the agency of materials and compared the creative process with divination: "Matter reveals secrets, it has its own genius; it is through matter that the oracle will speak."[11] Art Nouveau was crucial in disseminating the "true to the materials" aesthetic *[Materialgerechtigkeit]* that would dominate much of the thought about art, craft, and design in the first half of the twentieth century.[12] Not surprisingly: the artistic materials, then still by and large of natural origin, were seen as part of the agency of nature, and they contained the "laws"—in the form of technical and expressive properties—meant to dictate or at least suggest their own uses, like the mediums who, under the influence of magnetism or hypnosis, indicated the way in which they had to be treated.[13] Nature was generally conceived as in the feminine gender, and the same ambiguities or ambivalences of agency can be observed in the relationship between the artist and nature as between the physician and his patients, especially hysterics. The *cause célèbre* opposing Hippolyte Bernheim's theory of "suggestion" to Jean-Martin Charcot's belief in the objective existence of hysteria led to the recognition of the physician's influence upon the patients.[14] In the case of art, one would have to wait until the Surrealists to see anyone valorize the uncontrollable (in the guise of *écriture automatique*) to the point of negating the artist's active and conscious participation—and even then, with results that André Breton himself would describe as a "continuous misfortune."[15]

Around 1900, it was a question of deciphering, exploiting, and magnifying the artistic potential of each material, as can be seen with ceramics (see pp. 88/89) or glass (fig. 2). In his review of the 1889 Exposition Universelle, Gauguin criticized the use of different temperatures on the same ceramic in the name of an integrated agency: "And see how nature is an artist. The colors obtained in the same fire are always in harmony."[16] He condemned the application of paint or gilding to iron, asking for an "imposing construction suggestive of melting metal," and concluded with a manifesto of medium specificity: "Sculpture in ceramics, like

2 Louis Comfort Tiffany, Flower-shaped Ornamental Glass, 1905
Blown, iridescent glass, 31 × 12.8 × 11.8 cm
Museum für Gestaltung Zürich, Kunstgewerbesammlung

design, must be modeled 'in harmony with the material' [...] Plaster, wood, marble, bronze, and terracotta cannot be modeled in the same way, since each material has its different character of solidity, of hardness, of aspect."[17] This approach is evident in his own use of clay coil instead of the potter's wheel, and in the semi-accidental effects of glazing, such as the red dripping, evoking blood in his *Self-Portrait Jug* of the same year (fig. 3). Japanese tea ceremony *raku* ceramics, introduced into Europe at the 1878 Exposition Universelle, were instrumental in launching Jean Carriès's experiments with sandstone, glazes, and above all fire. In 1898, Louis Gonse commented on the then current influence of Japanese art by explaining that "for the Japanese, ceramics has to rise to the rank of natural chemistry with fire as its principal agent, and it must create objects the brilliance, beauty, and sumptuousness of which rival the works of nature itself."[18]

Analogous observations can be made about the use of wood, glass, and metal in Art Nouveau objects. Emile Gallé described his interaction with materials as a "fabrication of accidents" resulting in "small baroque problems posed to the imagination by the variegated material."[19] The culmination of this encounter may be his *Hand with Algae and Shells* (fig. 4), in which the enchantment of translucent glass and dynamic form glosses over the somewhat sinister subject of human life dissolving into a vegetal, submarine environment. A critic had written of an earlier work by Gallé that it was "the soul of wood bringing forth its memories to the dreamer's eyes."[20] In the case of wood, the traces of the shape of the living tree, and the presence of veins, imprint the material with a

3 Paul Gauguin, *Self-Portrait Jug* (*Pot en forme de tête, autoportrait*), 1889
Stoneware, ht: 19.3 cm, The Danish Museum of Decorative Art, Copenhagen
4 Emile Gallé, *Hand with Algae and Shells* (*La main aux algues et aux coquillages*), 1904
Crystal in several layers: partly blown, molded, modeled under heat, with inclusions,
applications, and wheel engraving, 33.4 × 13.4 cm, Musée d'Orsay, Paris
5 Josef Hoffmann, Palais Stoclet, Brussels, Column Hall, 1905–11
Photo: 1910, silver gelatin, 40 × 50 cm
Kaiser Wilhelm Museum, Krefeld, Sammlung "Deutsches Museum für Kunst in Handel und Gewerbe"

memory and with an "intention." Precisely at this time, participants in
the "renaissance" of woodcut such as Félix Vallotton renounced the
homogeneity of the assemblage of pieces of hard wood used for wood
engraving in favor of the plank, which brings with itself a resistant
pattern of its own. A wooden cup (fig. 6), cut around 1895 by Hermann
Obrist from the root of a tropical tree, similarly emphasizes the natural
structure of the material and extrapolates it into sculptural forms of
dynamic eddies.

A more direct integration of natural patterns was effected by the use
of veined stone (most commonly marble) for the facing of interior and
exterior walls. This technique had a long tradition going back to Antiquity and had been employed for its suggestive virtues in Byzantine,
Renaissance, and Baroque churches and palaces. It plays an important
role in the interior of Josef Hoffmann's Palais Stoclet in Brussels (fig. 5),
together with the geometric grid of the architecture and Gustav Klimt's
figurative frieze and abstract mosaics. This use of a "natural" decoration
was taken over and employed to great effect by architects who rejected
Art Nouveau and ornament, starting with Adolf Loos in his 1909–11
Haus am Michaelerplatz in Vienna. The short-lived episode of Art Nouveau architecture may thus have developed long-term effects in hidden
or disguised forms. As for metal, its ductility predestined it for the three-

6 Hermann Obrist, Wooden Cup, ca. 1895. Subtropical wood, 14 × 40 cm
Museum für Gestaltung Zürich, Kunstgewerbesammlung

dimensional visualization of structural dynamism. We have seen that Gauguin wished iron to be "suggestive of melting metal," that is, to evoke in its final, cooled-down form the fluid moment in which it was taking shape. This may be an echo of the observation made by Joris-Karl Huysmans, in reference to the ruins left by the Communards, that "fire is the essential artist of our time and that the architecture of the [nineteenth] century, so pitiful when it is raw, becomes imposing, almost splendid, when it is cooked." [21] It expressed in any case the turn-of-the-century love of shapes suspended in an inchoative state, *in statu nascendi*. Silver- and goldsmiths thus emulated fluidity, occasionally revisiting the early seventeenth-century Dutch auricular style *[Ohren-muschelstil]*. [22] Antoni Gaudí's collaborator Josep Maria Jujol thus made the wrought-iron elements of La Pedrera (fig. 7) visualize the process that gave them shape, and the British sculptor Alfred Gilbert emulated the fleeting aspects of flames in his bronze chimneypiece A Dream of Joy during a Sleep of Sorrow (fig. 8). Stone was more difficult to use in such a way, but the principle of medium specificity would lead to the sculp-

7 Josep Maria Jujol, detail of the wrought-iron entrance door to La Pedrera (Casa Milà),
architect: Antoni Gaudí, 1905–10, Barcelona
8 Alfred Gilbert, A Dream of Joy during a Sleep of Sorrow
(Sam Wilson chimneypiece), ca. 1908–14. Bronze (detail), 340 × 170.5 × 57 cm
Leeds City Art Gallery
9 Antoni Gaudí, Hydraulic Pavement, 1906–12. Reconstruction 2003, Passeig de Gràcia, Barcelona

tors' return to direct cutting. Rodin, who reached heights of inchoative
form in his *Gates of Hell* destined for bronze, established another endur-
ing *topos* by contrasting his polished figures with the raw marble from
which they emerge.

ORNAMENT, PROCESS, AND GROWTH

In 1856, Owen Jones opened his *Grammar of Ornament* by defining the
"desire for ornament" as common to all people and increasing "with all
in the ratio of their progress in civilisation"; his first illustration was of a
tattooed female head from New Zealand, which he regarded as "showing that in this very barbarous practice the principles of the very highest
oriental art are manifest, every line upon the face [being] the best adapted to develop the natural features."[23] Art Nouveau artists and designers
similarly revered ornament, and questioned the distinction and hierar-
chy between the fine and the applied or decorative arts. For a few decades ending—provisionally—with the interbellum opposition between
"pure" abstraction and figuration, decoration was seen as the prime
model for a non-mimetic form of representation. Like the Maori tattoo
admired by Jones, ornament tended to be restricted to the surface or
"skin" of things. But it could manifest their inner structure or inherent
vital principle by way of its shape, iconography, or sheer proliferation;
and it could challenge the distinction between surface and structure,

the contingent and the essential, in works as varied as Aubrey Beardsley's line drawings, Hector Guimard's cast-iron entrances to the Paris metro (see fig. 14 and see pp. 94/95), and Louis Sullivan's tall office buildings.[24]

Antoni Gaudí thus created a pavement (fig. 9)—strongly reminiscent of Ernst Haeckel's plates of maritime creatures (see pp. 24/25)—able to cover an unlimited area with a continuously expanding, radiating, or pulsating skin. The hexagonal tiles are designed in such a way that the centres of three distinct patterns are situated at three of their corners, so that the eye is ceaselessly drawn to move further across their surface. The love of dynamism explains the Art Nouveau predilection for the arabesque and the serpentine line (see pp. 90/91), of which William Hogarth had noted that its "intricacy of form" gives pleasure to the mind because it "leads the eye to a wanton kind of chase."[25] Such age-old observations assumed a radically new significance at a time when physics discovered waves at a level of natural phenomena inaccessible to the human senses—a fact that further legitimized the dictum "like nature, not after nature." Energy could be understood in a psychological, psychic, or even spiritual sense, as well as in a physical one, as made clear by "photographs of the soul," like those by Hippolyte Baraduc (fig. 10), which tend to resort to the visual language of waves and vortices.

The move away from the iconic depiction of external appearances also coincided with the exploration of the expressive properties of visual means. Charles Blanc revived Humbert de Superville's notion of "unconditional signs" in his 1867 *Grammaire des arts du dessin,* and architects, artists, and theoreticians such as August Endell promoted in Munich an "art of form" *[Formkunst]* that would neither derive from life study nor attempt to describe nature, but be a direct expression of the imagination.[26] Endell recognized that "it is difficult to avoid echoes of natural creations given the wealth of natural shapes," and the façade of his Munich photography studio Atelier Elvira (see pp. 92/93) demonstrates that he knew how to turn this difficulty to his advantage: the pattern is richer in kinetic suggestions (upward movement, winding course, lateral expansion) and in iconic ones (wave, fish-tail, leaf, shell, cracked earth, tongue, horn, hair) for not letting itself be reduced to any one of these identifications.

But the most important natural prototype remained the plant and especially the stem (fig. 11).[27] Why is this so? In addition to the many his-

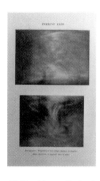  

10 *Psychicons: Projection of a State of Soul; Images of Haunting*, plate 23 from Hippolyte Baraduc,
L'âme humaine: Ses mouvements, ses lumières et l'iconographie de l'invisible fluidique, Paris, 1896
11 "Snowdrop", from: J. D. Ros, *Het ontwerpen van vlakornament* (The design of flat ornament),
Rotterdam, 1905, p. 82
12 Edouard Vuillard, *Le Corsage rayé (Woman in a Striped Dress)*, 1895
Oil on canvas, 65.7 × 58.7 cm
Washington, National Gallery of Art, Collection of Mr. and Mrs. Paul Mellon, Washington

torical reasons going back to ornamental traditions and to Goethe's
morphology, an important motive may be that the shape of plants not
only results from their growth, but keeps track of its progress: plants
are both the product and the image of their evolution, or, to put it the
other way round, the process of their growth can be retraced and stays
alive in their shape. To coin a phrase paying homage both to Henri
Focillon—an art theoretician and historian deeply indebted to Art Nouveau—and to his pupil George Kubler, one can say that plants make "the
shape of life" itself visible.[28] This "genemorphic" quality was bound
to appeal to the late-nineteenth-century fascination with generative
processes, informed as it was by the natural sciences. It is especially
close to Haeckel's biogenetic law, according to which "ontogenesis
recapitulates phylogenesis," and more precisely to the plates in which
Haeckel attempted to demonstrate, with the help of comparative embryology, that the individual retraces the evolutionary path not only of
its species, but of all species.[29] The identification of life as an all-perme-
ating, dynamic principle was also supported by the philosophy of Henri
Bergson, whose notion of *durée* emphasized the temporality of all
phenomena and valorized the emergence of the new in a way comparable to the Art Nouveau cult of youth, expressed for instance in the term
Jugendstil (style of youth) or in the title of the journal *Ver Sacrum*
(Sacred Spring). The organicism inherent in this biological paradigm

manifested itself at all levels, from the conception of artistic creation to the shape of objects to the understanding of historical processes such as the evolution of cities. In his groundbreaking treatise *City Planning According to Artistic Principles,* the Viennese architect and art historian Camillo Sitte criticized the modern cities designed on the drawing table and defended the plans—especially the irregular squares—which "had formed themselves little by little *in natura.*" [30]

EMPATHY

Art Nouveau objects of all sorts and sizes were conceived with the receiver in mind according to an "aesthetic of the effect" *[Wirkungs-ästhetik].* Arthur Mackmurdo wrote that "strength of imagination tells in favour of what we may best call subjective art, with both painter and spectator," and we have seen Endell resorting to "potential images," that is, images suggested by the work but depending on the viewer's imaginative perception to become actual. [31] The Art Nouveau interest in the decorative arts and in the interior as *Gesamtkunstwerk* may have been reinforced by the wish to develop aesthetic communication at a subliminal level, to exert a sort of capillary action upon the beholder as inhabitant of the artwork. The Symbolist poet and critic André Fontainas thus perceptively wrote that "the decorative work perpetually provokes a meditation ignorant of itself, a growth, a continuous ripening of the thinking being within ourselves," and he advocated a decoration "sufficiently vague and floating" so as not to define or circumscribe "this terrain of our psychic activity" too narrowly. [32] The echo of contemporary psychological research is again unmistakable, and one can think of the decorations painted by Edouard Vuillard for his friends Misia and Thadée Natanson (fig. 12), with their oscillation between figure and ground, and their seamless weaving of wallpaper, flowers, and dress fabrics. [33]

The organic shapes cultivated by Art Nouveau appealed to the embodied vision analyzed by French theorists of *suggestion* like Paul Souriau and Gabriel Séailles, and by the German aestheticians of "empathy" *[Einfühlung].* For Theodor Lipps, for instance, empathy was connected to the "anthropomorphic tendency [...] arising directly from the likeness between the shapes and movements we observe in nature and those

13 Th. Th. Heine, drawing, in: Meier-Gräfe, *Loie Fuller*, from: Otto Julius Bierbaum, Alfred Walther Heymel, and Rudolf Alexander Schröder, eds., *Die Insel* (April to June) Berlin, 1900, p. 102
14 Hector Guimard, entrance to the Métropolitain,
Palais Royal—Musée du Louvre station, Paris, 1900, cast-iron
15 Brassaï, *Mange-moi !*, Métro Modern Style, 1933, from: *Minotaure* (No. 3–4) Paris 1933, p. 75

we produce or discover in ourselves"; it was not an arbitrary projection but the discovery that objects have a life *[Lebendigkeit]*, and consisted in an "inner participation" in the "expressive movement" perceived in them.[34] Although such theories claimed a universal validity, they clearly have a special relevance for the art and design of their time: in front of an Art Nouveau lamp, desk, chimney-piece, or façade, and provided we respond to its suggestions, we inwardly bend down, gather ourselves up, rise, and turn on ourselves, unfolding a temporal act of perception that is not only visual but tactile, kinetic, and even somatic—a sort of Loie Fuller dance of the mind (fig. 13). Following Fontainas's advice, this can be best experienced within a home, resting on a couch or in an armchair, and it is significant that these two instruments of domestic relaxation were promoted, within a few decades, by Freud to the rank of instrument of the psychoanalytical cure, and by Matisse to that of metaphor of the ideal work of art.[35]

Such indulgence, however, could appear regressive, and it expectedly attracted criticism. The Art Nouveau preference for soft, fluid, and even "amorphous" shapes was regarded by some as expressing and advocating a loosening of moral control; a conservative critic thus denounced the "lascivious forms" and "pornographic provocation" of Guimard, whose lamps crowning the Metro entrances (fig. 14) he saw as "the most unbearable public representation of the female sex."[36] Such a diagnosis called for a return to the "virile" orthogonal grid that would be radicalized by the Modern movement. Abstraction was very much a part of Art Nouveau, as were geometric forms, especially the dynamic spiral; but it did not shun the possibility of an iconic link—generative or associative—with nature. In his 1907 doctoral dissertation *Abstraktion und Einfühlung*, Wilhelm Worringer attempted on the contrary to sever this link by claiming that the "original urge to make art" *[Urkunsttrieb]* was not the "need for empathy," but the independent and superior "need for abstraction." He questioned Alois Riegl's derivation of the Islamic arabesque from plant ornament, and claimed that geometric abstraction, corresponding to the postulation of transcendence in monotheistic religion, was superior to the sensualist *Einfühlung*, anthropomorphism, and naturalism. As for the references to the creations of "primitive people" and children, he rejected them as extraneous to art proper.[37] Similarly, Loos turned the association with the primitive against ornament, although we have seen that he continued to employ it in the surreptitious form of natural patterns.[38]

This going into hiding is typical of the fate of Art Nouveau during the first half of the twentieth century, and it was accompanied by much destruction, especially in architecture. An early contributor to its rediscovery, Salvador Dalí, had the advantage of being born and raised in Catalonia, where Art Nouveau, in the guise of the local Modernisme, had remained a living force into the 1920s.[39] In 1933, Dalí published in the French Surrealist journal *Minotaure* an article devoted to "Modern' Style architecture" with photographs by Man Ray and Brassaï. Dalí found in Art Nouveau architecture, especially by Gaudí, manifestations of the "paranoiac" capacity of the human imagination to shape the world according to its desires. Nature could only provide it with stimuli, and the image of a stone from Cap de Creus—a natural curiosity that had fascinated him since childhood—was captioned as an "attempt at geological Modern' Style, a failure like all that comes from fanciless nature."[40] In the forms of Casa Battló, Casa Milà, and the Parc Güell, he found "fossilizations" of fleeting aspects of the psychic and the natural world such as waves, clouds, foam, or smoke. Empathy was for him more than a possibility, an obligation, and he could hear the shoots of Guimard's Metro entrances whisper to him: "Eat me!" (fig. 15).

1 See, for instance, James Engell, *The Creative Imagination: Enlightenment to Romanticism*, Cambridge, Mass., 1981.

2 Siegfried Bing, "L'Art Nouveau", in *The Craftsman*, vol. 5 (October 1903), p. 3, quoted in *Art Nouveau: Art and Design at the Turn of the Century*, ed. Peter Selz and Mildred Constantine, exh. cat., The Museum of Modern Art, New York, 1960, p. 14; letter of August 13, 1894, from August Strindberg to Leopold Littmansson, in *August Strindbergs brev*, vol. 10, Stockholm, 1968, p. 215. On Bing, see *Les origines de l'Art Nouveau: La maison Bing*, ed. Gabriel P. Weisberg, Edwin Becker, and Evelyne Possémé, exh. cat., Van Gogh Museum, Amsterdam, Musée des arts décoratifs, Paris and Antwerp, 2004.

3 See Friedrich Weltzien, ed., *Von selbst: Autopoietische Verfahren in der Ästhetik des 19. Jahrhunderts*, Berlin, 2006.

4 See August Strindberg, "The New Arts! or The Role of Chance in Artistic Creation" [1894], trans. Michael Robinson, in *Selected Essays by August Strindberg*, Cambridge, 1996, pp. 103 07.

5 Paul Gauguin, *Oviri: Écrits d'un sauvage* [1889], ed. Daniel Guérin, Paris, 1974, p. 59; compare the statement by Schinkel quoted in Barry Bergdoll's essay.

6 Alfred Gell, *Art and Agency: An Anthropological Theory*, Oxford, 1998.

7 Kenneth J. Arrow, "Agency and the Market", in *Handbook of Mathematical Economics*, III, ed. K. J. Arrow and Michael D. Intriligator, Amsterdam, 1986, pp. 1183–95.

8 See Debora L. Silverman, *Art Nouveau in Fin-de-Siècle France: Politics, Psychology, and Style*, Berkeley, 1989.

9 *Dessins de Victor Hugo*, Paris, 1863, p. 7. ["les chimères de la fantaisie & les caprices fortuits de la main inconsciente"]

10 Letter of August 16, 1898, from Odilon Redon to André Mellerio, in *Lettres d'Odilon Redon 1878–1916*, Paris and Brussels, 1923, pp. 33–34.

11 Odilon Redon, *A soi-même: Journal (1867–1915) – Notes sur la vie, l'art et les artistes*, Paris, 1979, p. 128 [1913].

12 See Günter Bandmann, "Der Wandel der Materialbewertung in der Kunsttheorie des 19. Jahrhunderts", in *Beiträge zur Theorie der Künste im 19. Jahrhundert*, ed. Helmut Koopmann and J. Adolf Schmoll gen. Eisenwerth, Frankfurt am Main, 1971, pp. 129–57.

13 See for example Justinus Kerner, *Die Seherin von Prevorst: Eröffnungen über das innere Leben des Menschen und über das Hereinragen einer Geisterwelt in die unsere*, Stuttgart, 1829.

14 See Robert G. Hillman, "A Scientific Study of Mystery: The Role of the Medical and Popular Press in the Nancy-Salpêtrière Controversy on Hypnotism", in *Bulletin of the History of Medicine*, vol. 39 (1965), pp. 163–82.

15 André Breton, "Le message automatique", in *Minotaure*, no. 3–4 (1933), pp. 55–65.

16 Paul Gauguin, "Notes sur l'art: L'exposition universelle", in *Le Moderniste illustré*, July 4/11, 1889, quoted after Gauguin, *Oviri*, pp. 47–52. ["Et voyez comme la nature est artiste. Les couleurs obtenues dans un même feu sont toujours en harmonie."]

17 Ibid., pp. 51–2. ["une construction imposante et suggestive du métal en fusion"; "La sculpture, comme le dessin, dans la céramique, doit aussi être modelée 'harmoniquement avec la matière'... Le plâtre, le bois, le marbre, le bronze et l'argile cuite ne doivent pas être modelés de la même façon, attendu que chaque matière a un caractère différent de solidité, de dureté, d'aspect."]

18 Louis Gonse, "L'art japonais et son influence sur le goût européen", in *Revue des Arts décoratifs* (April 1898), pp. 112–15, quoted in *Le Japonisme*, exh. cat., Galeries nationales du Grand Palais, Paris, Musée national d'art occidental, Tokyo, Paris, 1998, pp. 138–9. ["aux yeux des Japonais, la céramique doit s'élever au rang d'une chimie naturelle, dont l'agent principal est le feu et qui doit créer des objets dont l'éclat, la beauté et la somptuosité rivaliseront avec œuvres de la nature elle-même"]

19 Emile Gallé, *Écrits pour l'art: Floriculture – Art décoratif – Notices d'exposition (1884–89)* [1908], Marseille, 1998, p. 350 ["une fabrication d'accidents qui deviennent... de petits problèmes baroques posés par la matière bigarrée à l'imagination"]

20 Louis de Fourcaud, "Les arts décoratifs au Salon de 1892", in *Revue des arts décoratifs*, vol. 13 (1892–93), pp. 1–14. ["C'est l'âme du bois extériorisant ses souvenances aux yeux du rêveur"]

21 J.-K. Huysmans, "Fantaisie sur le Musée des arts décoratifs et sur l'architecture cuite", in *Revue indépendante*, n.s., no. 1 (November 1886), reprinted in J.-K. Huysmans, *Certains* [1889], Paris, 1975, pp. 397–9.

22 See James Trilling, *The Language of Ornament*, London, 2001, pp. 66–7, 203–9; Dario Gamboni, "Eine Perle in der Ohrenmuschel: Bewegung, Prozess, Einfühlung", in *Über Grenzen – Kunstvermittlungen: Festschrift Antje von Graevenitz*, ed. Renate Goldmann et al, Berlin, 2006, pp. 31–36.

23 Owen Jones, *The Grammar of Ornament Illustrated by Examples from Various Styles of Ornament* [1856], Paris, 2001, p. 15.

24 See David Van Zanten, *Sullivan's City: The Meaning of Ornament for Louis Sullivan*, New York and London, 2000.

25 William Hogarth, *The Analysis of Beauty* [1753], ed. Ronald Paulson, New Haven and London, 1997, pp. 32–35; see also Werner Busch, *Die notwendige Arabeske: Wirklichkeitsaneignung und Stilisierung in der deutschen Kunst des 19. Jahrhunderts*, Berlin, 1985; and Susanne Deicher, ed., *Die weibliche und die männliche Linie: Das imaginäre Geschlecht der modernen Kunst von Klimt bis Mondrian*, Berlin, 1993.

26 August Endell, "Architektonische Erstlinge", in *Dekorative Kunst*, vol. 3, no. 8 (May 1900), pp. 314–15, quoted in Peg Weiss, *Kandinsky in Munich: The Formative Jugendstil Years*, Princeton, 1979, p. 35; see also Jean-Paul Bouillon, *Journal de l'Art Nouveau 1870–1914*, Geneva, 1985, p. 123.

27 See Leïla el-Wakil, "Art Nouveau et nature: Quelques réflexions autour de la forme en architecture", in *Mélanges en l'honneur du prof. Marcel Roethlisberger,* Geneva and Milan, forthcoming.
28 See Henri Focillon, *Vie des formes*, Paris, 1934; George Kubler, *The Shape of Time: Remarks on the History of Things,* New Haven and London, 1962; Dario Gamboni, "De Bernheim à Focillon: la notion de suggestion entre médecine, esthétique, critique et histoire de l'art", in *L'histoire de l'histoire de l'art en France au XIXe siècle,* ed. Roland Recht, Paris, forthcoming.
29 Ernst Haeckel, *Anthropogenie, oder Entwicklungsgeschichte des Menschen,* Leipzig, 1874; on Haeckel's manipulation of anatomic evidence, see Michael K. Richardson et al, "There Is No Highly Conserved Embryonic Stage in the Vertebrates: Implications for Current Theories of Evolution and Development", in *Anatomy and Embryology,* vol. 196, no. 2 (August 1997), pp. 91–106.
30 Camillo Sitte, *Der Städte-Bau nach seinen künstlerischen Grundsätzen,* Vienna, 1889, chapter 5.
31 Arthur H. Mackmurdo, "The Guild's Flag Unfurling", in *Hobby Horse,* vol. 1 (1884), pp. 1–13, quoted after Henri Dorra, ed., *Symbolist Art Theories: A Critical Anthology,* Berkeley, 1994, pp. 96–97; see Dario Gamboni, *Potential Images: Ambiguity and Indeterminacy in Modern Art,* London, 2002, esp. pp. 18–20, 119–22.
32 André Fontainas, *Notes et scolies*, unpublished notes, pp. 124–25, entry of February 24, 1895, quoted in Laurent Houssais, *André Fontainas (1865–1948) critique et historien de l'art,* Ph.D. dissertation, Université Blaise-Pascal Clermont II, 2003, p. 422. ["l'œuvre décorative est un provoquant perpétuel à une méditation qui s'ignore, à un accroissement, à un *mûrissement* continu de l'être en nous qui pense… il ne faut pas que ce terrain de notre activité psychique soit trop défini, circonscrit… une décoration plus vague, flottante."]
33 See Gloria Groom, *Edouard Vuillard Painter-Decorator: Patrons and Projects, 1892–1912*, New Haven and London, 1993.
34 Theodor Lipps, *Ästhetik: Psychologie des Schönen und der Kunst,* Leipzig and Hamburg, 1914, 1:111, 163–67, 206–07; see Harry Francis Mallgrave and Eleftherios Ikonomou, eds., *Empathy, Form, and Space: Problems in German Aesthetics, 1873–1893,* Santa Monica, 1994.
35 See *Die Couch: Vom Denken im Liegen,* ed. Lydia Marinelli, exh. cat., Sigmund Freud Museum Vienna, Munich, 2006; Henri Matisse, "Notes d'un peintre" [1908], in H. Matisse, *Écrits et propos sur l'art.*, ed. Dominique Fourcade, Paris, 1972, p. 50.
36 Anonymous, "La provocation pornographique de MM. Guimard et Bénard", *La Croix* (March 17, 1902), quoted in el-Wakil, "Art Nouveau et nature", op. cit. ["la représentation la plus odieusement insupportable du sexe féminin"]
37 Wilhelm Worringer, *Abstraktion und Einfühlung: Ein Beitrag zur Stilpsychologie* [1908], Dresden, 1996, esp. pp. 76, 81–84, 92–94, 109–10, 146–48.
38 Adolf Loos, "Ornament und Verbrechen" [1908], in A. Loos, *Ins Leere gesprochen*, vol. 1, *Sämtliche Schriften,* Vienna and Munich, 1962, pp. 276–88; see Brent C. Brolin, *Flight of Fancy: The Banishment and Return of Ornament,* London, 1985.
39 See Mireia Freixa, "Modern' Style i Dalí: algunes consideracions", in *Salvador Dalí i les arts: Historiografia i crítica al segle XXI,* ed. Lourdes Cirlot and Mercè Vidal, Barcelona, 2005, pp. 89–96.
40 Salvador Dalí, "De la beauté terrifiante et comestible, de l'architecture Modern' Style", in *Minotaure,* no. 3–4 (1933), pp. 69–76. ["Essai de Modern' Style géologique, raté comme tout ce qui vient de la nature privée d'imagination"]

TOI

OGRAPHY

Zaha Hadid, Z-Scape Furniture: Moraine Divan, 2000
Fireproof foam, leather, 338 × 120 × 75 cm
Sawaya & Moroni Spa, Milan, IT

Zaha Hadid, Z-Scape Furniture: Glacier Bench, 2000
Two combinable individual parts, wood with lacquer finish,
500 × 125 × 48 cm
Sawaya & Moroni Spa, Milan, IT

Zaha Hadid's Z-Scape furniture, of which to date the
pieces *Glacier, Moraine, Stalactite,* and *Stalagmite* have
been realized (the latter two are tables and are not shown),
are planned as an integrated program comprised of
eleven individual elements, a landscape measuring
500 × 350 × 75 cm that, as per necessity, can be assembled,
like a puzzle, in distinct ways. Z-Scape, like Hadid's
architecture (pp. 234–39), frequently references the topography, the forms of the landscape—in this case glaciers
and soil erosion—which are integrated into elements,
and which, though flowing, define a clear trace. They are
later formed either as hard elements with planar surfaces
or as soft seating elements.

Ronan and Erwan Bouroullec, Stone Vase (Vase Caillou), 2002
Porcelain, 9 × 16 × 18 cm
Ronan and Erwan Bouroullec, commissioned by the Délégation
aux Arts Plastiques, Ministère de la Culture, FR

Jens-Flemming Sørensen, Globe Porcelain Bowl, 2005
Porcelain, diameter: 18 cm
Royal Copenhagen A/S, Glostrup, DK

Marcel Wanders, Splinter, 2001
Vase. Crystal, 15 × 15 × 15 cm
Moooi B.V., Breda, NL

Harry Bertoia, Diamond Chair, 1952/53
Steel frame, wire seat basket, textile cushion, 72 × 114 × 80 cm
Knoll International. Museum für Gestaltung Zürich, Designsammlung

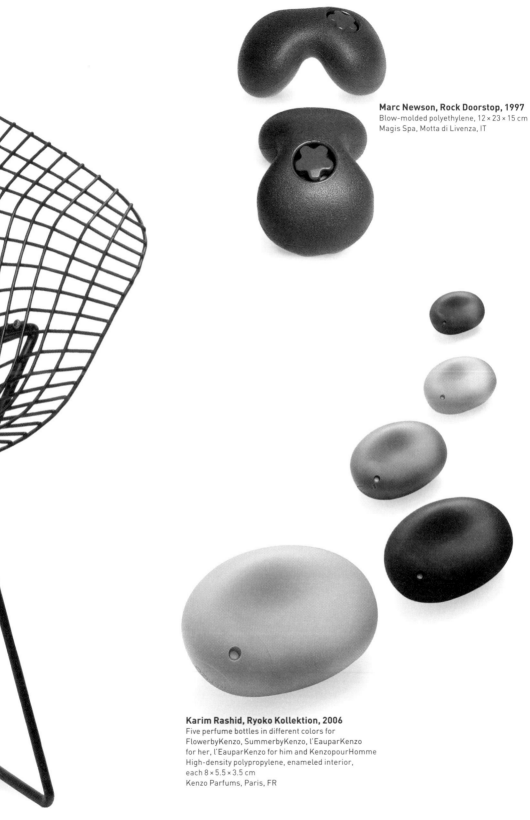

Marc Newson, Rock Doorstop, 1997
Blow-molded polyethylene, 12 × 23 × 15 cm
Magis Spa, Motta di Livenza, IT

Karim Rashid, Ryoko Kollektion, 2006
Five perfume bottles in different colors for
FlowerbyKenzo, SummerbyKenzo, l'EauparKenzo
for her, l'EauparKenzo for him and KenzopourHomme
High-density polypropylene, enameled interior,
each 8 × 5.5 × 3.5 cm
Kenzo Parfums, Paris, FR

Theodor Tobler, Emil Baumann, Toblerone, since 1908
Toblerone enamel plaque, ca. 1920, ca. 250×300 cm
Kraft Foods Schweiz AG, Zürich, CH

Developed in 1908, Toblerone is one of the best-known
and oldest brands in Switzerland, and is the only brand
of chocolate whose shape is legally protected. There
are two legends concerning its creation. The first
is based on the idea that the model for the triangular
form of Toblerone was provided by the Matterhorn. The
second says that the owner of the firm, Theodor Tobler,
found inspiration in a pyramid formed by the dancers
at the Folies Bergères, which he saw on one of his trips
to Paris. In both cases, nature provided the model.
This advertising sign from the heroic era of Toblerone,
however, suggests to us we should look for the inspiration in the Swiss mountains. Although the form of the
packaging has remained always the same, the details
have been regularly altered. The naturalistic depiction
of the Matterhorn with the word "Toblerone" beside
it has now been replaced by an abstract depiction of a
triangular, snow-covered mountain, with an edelweiss
and the company lettering.

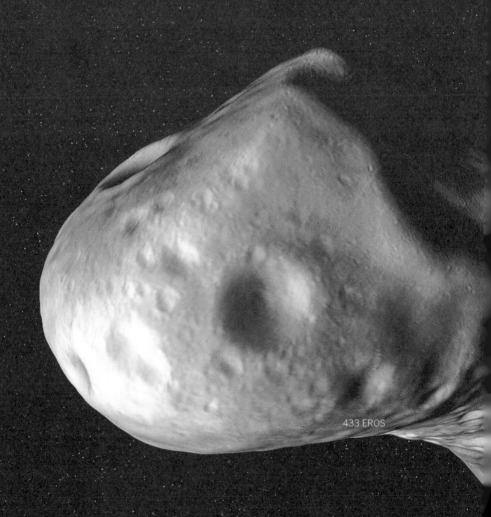

433 EROS

TERRA ·

Christian Waldvogel, *433 Eros:*
***Werkzeug zur Gesamtumgestaltung der Erde*, 2007**
433 Eros: Tool for the Complete Transformation of the Earth
Computer drawings, plan and elevation
Christian Waldvogel, Zurich, CH

The most extensive process of "Nature Design" to date occurred during the transition from the Cretaceous to the Tertiary period, when an asteroid the size of the city of Paris collided with the earth. The resulting release of energy changed the earth's climate and led to the extinction of the dinosaurs and many other species. This was the basis for evolution, the spread of the mammals, and the development of Man.

Since the end of the twentieth century, universities and space agencies have been recording astral objects that pose a potential threat to the earth; by the year 2008, 90 percent of those with a diameter of at least one kilometer will have been registered.

This research program is intended on the one hand to allow the threat posed by asteroids to be calculated, and on the other to develop scenarios in the case of a possible collision. Within the framework of this program, the probe NEAR Shoemaker measured the asteroid 433 Eros—originally discovered in 1898—that moves between the orbits of the Earth and the planet Mars. With a length of thirty-three kilometers, it is comparable to the one that so enduringly changed the earth 65.5 million years ago.

Christian Waldvogel understands *433 Eros* as representing the "global scalpel," and develops the scenario of a new collision at the beginning of the twenty-first century that affects the Zurich area. In the Museum für Gestaltung Zürich, *433 Eros* is exhibited as a 1:500 scale model. What is still imagination in the park penetrates the external wall of the museum and becomes visible in the exhibition space as a volume with a depth of thirty-five centimeters, corresponding in reality to a length of 175 meters.

Sources: 433 Eros 3D model: Arizona State University / NASA. 433 Eros surface texture: University of Maryland / NASA. Satellite photo and clouds, Zurich Region: The Blue Marble / NASA

MARS →

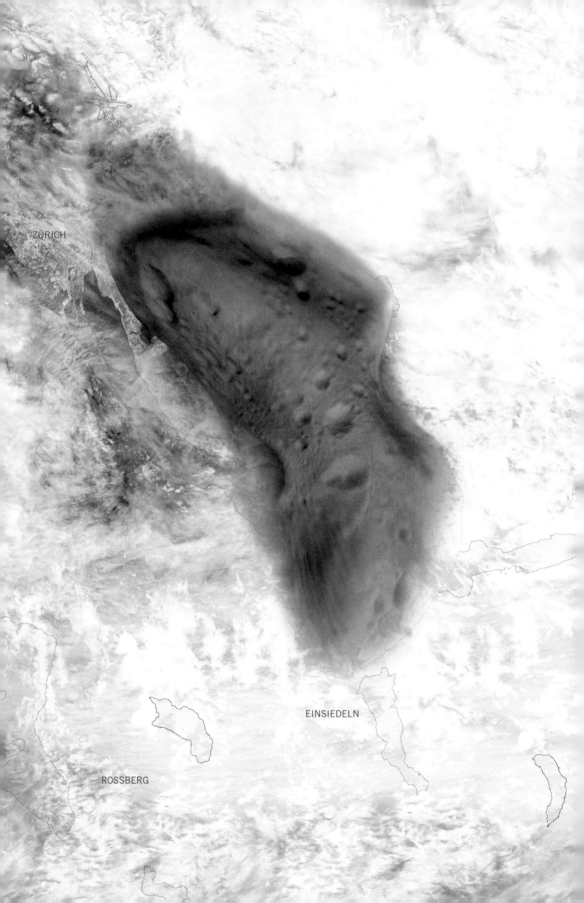

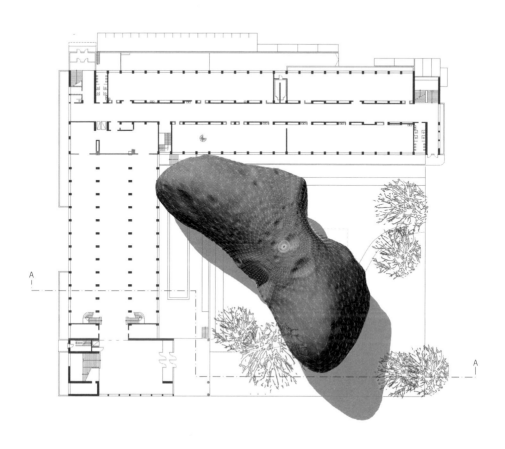

125

FOREST

Ines Schaber, Jörg Stollmann, *On movers and shapers*, 2001
Two photographs, 200 × 200 cm and 60 × 60 cm; DVD, 47 mins.
Ines Schaber, Berlin, DE, and Jörg Stollmann, Zurich, CH

In the Southwest United States, gated communities are a widespread form of residential development. Not only is access to them controlled, but they are also tied to a system of "codes, covenants & restrictions" that determines the external appearance of the residential community, thereby also shaping their aesthetic and social identity.

The desert was once regarded as uninhabitable, and thus, especially in the 1980s and 1990s, gated communities were generally not only shielded by the usual walls, but were also designed as shady tropical oases that contrasted sharply with their hostile surroundings. In the meantime,

the developers of such projects have begun to reflect on the original identity of the Southwest and the desert is now used as the model for the design of the exterior spaces in these developments. Taking up the principles of eighteenth-century English garden design, boundaries or obstacles do not interrupt sightlines, thus achieving a visual cohesion between private and public land. To make this subtle treatment possible, additional desert land is acquired. Whereas once the developments were fenced-in islands, today they have become outward reaching "view-spaces" that negate the outside world through a strategy of fading it out of the picture.

Olafur Eliasson, *The Madagascar Hall series*, 2005
9 photographs, 39 × 50 cm each
Private Collection

Günther Vogt (project by Kienast Vogt Partner), Masoala Rainforest
Hall, Zürich Zoo, Constructed Nature, 1994–2003
Vogt Landschaftsarchitekten AG, Zurich, CH

The Masoala Rainforest Hall is a national park with the
flora and fauna of Madagascar, but on Swiss territory.
It measures 120 × 90 meters and is roofed by a shell made
of steel and plastic reaching to a height of 30 meters.
That Madagascar was separated from the other continents
at an early stage means that nature developed independently, and a large percentage of its plants and animals are
only found there, and in that specific form.

These unique conditions were created in the constructed
nature of the Masoala Rainforest Hall in Zurich. This
jungle, like in Madagascar, is built up on three levels (tree
level, shrub level, and ground level). Following a winding
path with level changes that leads through the variety
of habitats in the rainforest—passing by waterfalls, lakes,
and marshes—visitors experience the landscape with
its native plants and animals. Birds and flying foxes glide
through the air, chameleons sit immobile at the side of
the path, lemurs leap from tree to tree.

In contrast to the typical zoological environment in
which visitors stroll past animal cages or open-air enclo-
sures, here they become part of nature, offering a unique
experience. Nevertheless, the question arises as to
why a natural habitat from Madagascar should have to
be recreated in Switzerland. The answer is that 96 percent
of the original wooded area of Madagascar has been
destroyed; the Masoala National Park in the northeast of
the island was set up only in 1997 after the start of the
Zurich initiative, and is partly financed by donations from
the Zürich Zoo. In this way, artificial nature is more
frequently playing a role in the protection of real nature.

Olafur Eliasson explored the Masoala Rainforest
Hall in an excursion and documented it, just as in some
of his work he has documented the natural spaces of his
native country, Iceland, and presented it in photographic
encyclopedias.

Richard Hutten, Dandelion, 2004
Pendant Lamp. Laser-cut,
powder-coated steel, 55 × 80 cm
Moooi B.V., Breda, NL

Poul Henningsen, PH Artichoke lamp, 1958
72 scales made of stainless steel, wet-enameled, 74 cm
Louis Poulsen. Vitra Design Museum, Weil am Rhein, DE

Werner Aisslinger, treelight, 2007
Lamp. Globe of laser-formed metal strips,
lacquered with a gold-finished interior.
Tripod and fixing polyurethane, double-butted
aluminum tubing, lacquered, 164 × 55 cm
DAB, Barcelona, ES

Karim Rashid, Cadmo, 2006
Lamp. Painted steel, inox steel, 174 × 32 cm
Artemide Spa, Pregnana Milanese, IT

Nils Landberg,
Zwei Tulpengläser, 1954
Two tulip glasses. Colorless glass
with cloudy white or smoke
blue underlayer, mold-blown,
33.4 × 11.2 cm, 34.3 × 11.6 cm
Museum für Gestaltung Zürich,
Kunstgewerbesammlung

Matali Crasset, Transplant ≠ 01, ≠ 07, ≠ 05, ≠ 02, 2006/07
Containers, vases. Glass, mouth-blown, four rod elements in the vessel, ca. 60 × 29 × 29 cm,
60 × 29 × 29 cm, 67 × 27 × 27 cm, 63 × 20 × 20 cm; diameter depends on the variable position of the rods
Courtesy of Galleria Luisa delle Piane, Milan, IT. Matali Crasset, Paris, FR

Simone Stocker, torlo, 2002–05
Five-piece tableware set consisting of plate, soup dish,
bowl, cup, and beaker, porcelain, 3 × 30 cm, 6.6 × 23.8 cm,
8.7 × 18.2 cm, 9.5 × 11.2 cm, 9.2 × 4.6 cm
bottoni porzellan, Simone Stocker, Bern, CH

Torlo conveys the impression of an open blossom. It is based
on the basic geometric forms and mathematical laws of
growth, which also apply to nature. Each of the five pieces of
the set consists of three curves, two concave and one convex.

George Nelson, Coconut Chair, 1955
Shell of fiberglass-reinforced plastic, chromium steel
tubular frame, upholstered in leather, 83.5 × 104 × 83.5 cm
Vitra AG, Birsfelden, CH

René Lalique, Cactus, 1928
Perfume bottle. Colorless crystal glass, black
enamel. Globular body covered with a honeycomb
pattern of small drops or beads that grow
smaller and flatter towards the shoulder and
base. Short cylindrical neck. Stopper in the form
of an elongated hemisphere, also with drops.
Bottle from the dressing-table set Cactus that
was also produced in a 12 cm size until 1937.
In production again since 1947, 9.6 × 8.3 cm
Museum für Gestaltung Zürich,
Kunstgewerbesammlung

Philippe Starck, Juicy Salif, 1990
Lemon squeezer. Cast aluminum, 29 × 14 cm
Alessi Spa, Crusinallo, IT

Wilhelm Kienzle, Kakteen-Giesskanne, ca. 1935
Cactus watering-can. Tin plate, painted, 44 × 16 × 11 cm
Blattmann Metallwarenfabrik AG, MEWA, Wädenswil, CH.
Museum für Gestaltung Zürich, Designsammlung

Wieki Somers, Blossoms, 2004
Vase. Ceramic, glass tubes, 53 × 27 × 17 cm
Cor Unum contemporary ceramics, Den Bosch, NL

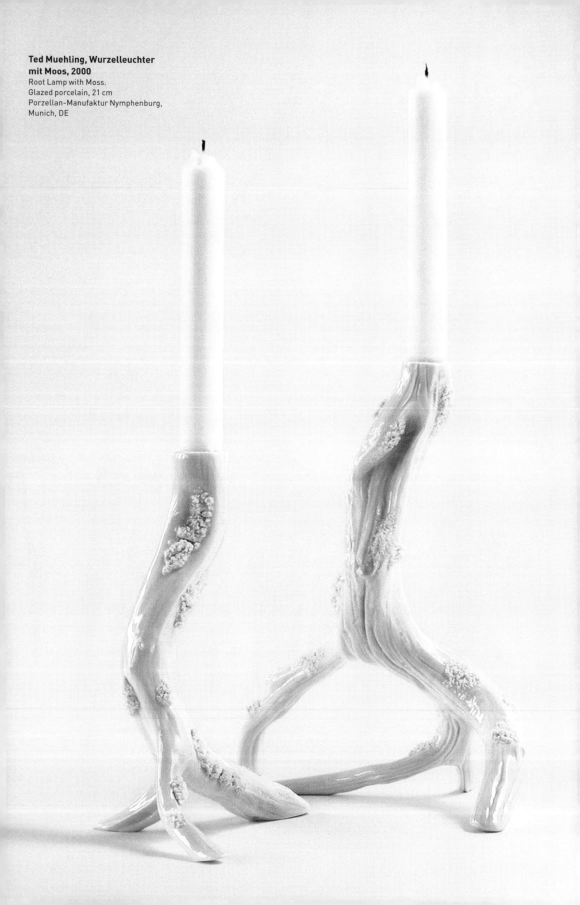

**Ted Muehling, Wurzelleuchter
mit Moos, 2000**
Root Lamp with Moss.
Glazed porcelain, 21 cm
Porzellan-Manufaktur Nymphenburg,
Munich, DE

Jürgen Mayer H., Karlsruhe Student Cafeteria, Fachhochschule, Pädagogische Hochschule und Kunstakademie Karlsruhe, 2004–07
J. Mayer H., Berlin, DE
Northeast and southwest façades
....
Conceptual diagram of the building "Nutellagramm"
....
Detail of external elevation
....
p. 144/145 Overall view from outside

The new student cafeteria in Karlsruhe, serving three different universities, is an elastic building at the center of the campus intended to mediate between the identities of the three institutions, the urban plan, and the Hardt forest. The permeable, forest-like structure of the sculptural building is based on the conceptual diagram of the threads formed by the filling of a sandwich as it is pulled apart. This "Nutellagramm" is then translated into architecture. The striking timber-built cafeteria is covered with a two-millimeter-thick, yellow-green polyurethane skin.

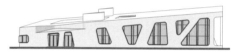

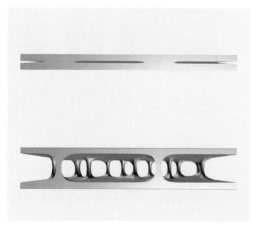

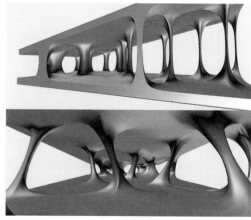

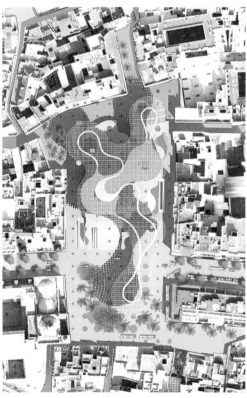

Jürgen Mayer H., Metropol Parasol,
Plaza de la Encarnación, Seville, ES, since 2004
J. Mayer H., Berlin, DE
View of Calle Imagen, looking northeast
....
Layout plan
....
Panorama route on the Metropol Parasol towards the north
....
View of the archaeological excavation site, the market,
and the elevated square of Calle Imagen

Through its redefinition with an organic, mushroom-like
architecture, Plaza de la Encarnación in the heart of
Seville is to become a contemporary city center, connecting
its cultural legacy with the revitalization of urban life and
leisure activity in the area. The mushrooms, covered with
polyurethane, have a timber structure and grow out of
the Roman-era archaeological finds that lie beneath them,
where a museum is being created. The mushrooms
form a new urban symbol that, alongside the activities,
conveys dynamic spatial experiences. The outward-
reaching structure provides shade, space for a market,
an elevated square for cultural events, numerous bars and
restaurants above and below the mushrooms, and a panorama deck on their surface, while the stems contain the
circulation infrastructure.

Tarnnetz, 1980
Camouflage Net. Polyamide, iron with anti-rust finish,
mixed fiber with anti-rot coating, 600 × 600 cm
Amt für Militär und Zivilschutz des Kantons Zürich, CH

Camouflage is a decisive strategy in nature, employed to
make a creature invisible to its enemies and thus protecting
its life. The most extreme form is mimicry, in which either
an animal deceptively imitates another so that it appears
more threatening than it actually is, or, like the Peppered
Moth—whose wings have a pattern so closely adapted to its
environment that it blends in with the background—it becomes almost invisible.
     The term camouflage derives from the military world,
and describes the measures outlined above that are used
to conceal soldiers, positions, machinery, vehicles, and
weaponry from the enemy. Camouflage nets that imitate a
canopy of leaves with a summer and autumn side are merely
one element of camouflage that extends to the soldiers'
uniforms and their equipment, and even to camouflage face
makeup. The use of the colors and forms of camouflage
in contemporary fashion is a barometer of global conflict.

1st Ave Machine, *Sixes Last*, for Anticon Records, 2005
Music video
1st Ave Machine, New York, US

In this music video, artificial natural elements inserted within real nature move to the beat of the music, producing a jungle filled with sound.

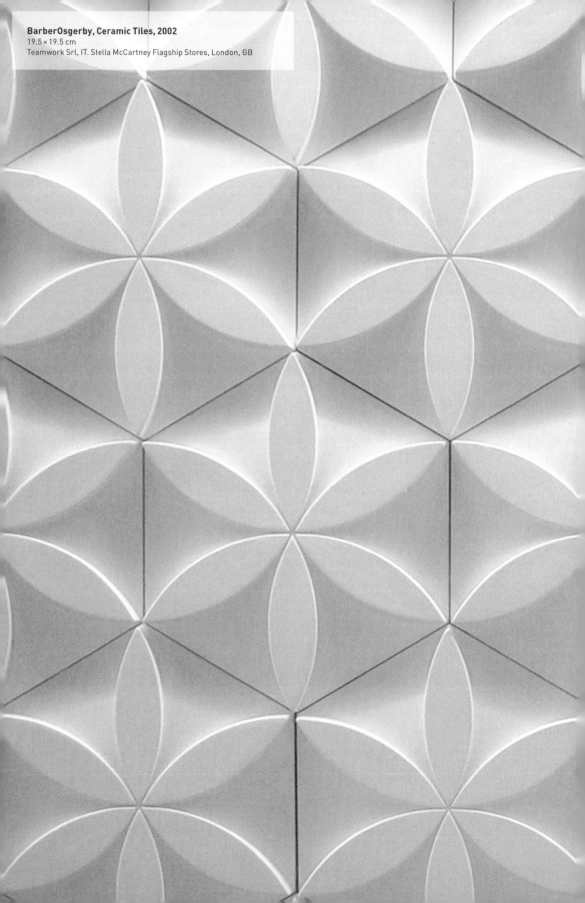

BarberOsgerby, Ceramic Tiles, 2002
19.5 × 19.5 cm
Teamwork Srl, IT. Stella McCartney Flagship Stores, London, GB

Barnaby Barford and Valeria Miglioli, StampCups, 2003
Set of two cups. Earthenware, 8.3 × 12.5 × 9.8 cm
thorsten van elten, London, GB

Susi+Ueli Berger, Schubladenstapel, 1981
Stacked Drawers. Plywood with diagonal palisander
veneer, 105 × 50 × 55 cm
Röthlisberger Schreinerei AG, Gümligen, CH.
Museum für Gestaltung Zürich, Designsammlung

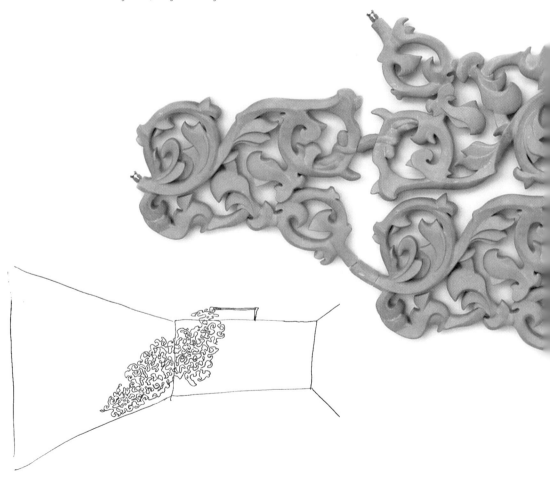

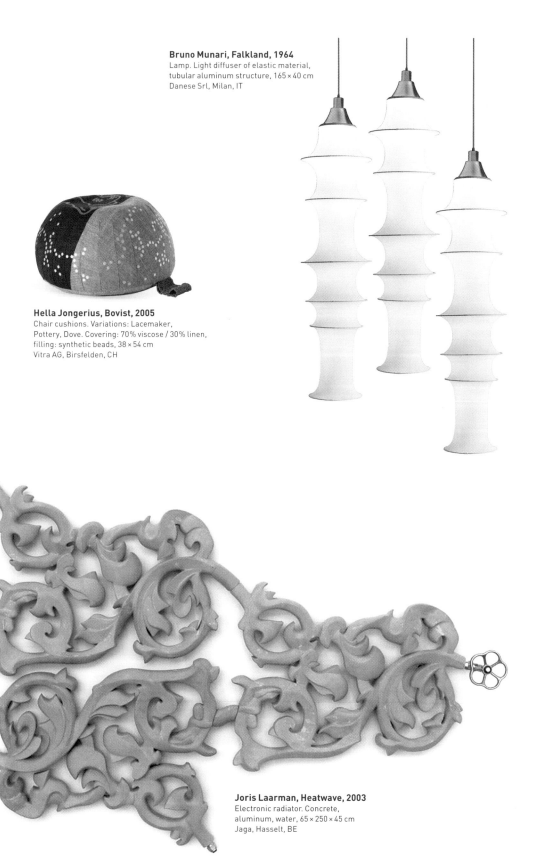

Bruno Munari, Falkland, 1964
Lamp. Light diffuser of elastic material,
tubular aluminum structure, 165 × 40 cm
Danese Srl, Milan, IT

Hella Jongerius, Bovist, 2005
Chair cushions. Variations: Lacemaker,
Pottery, Dove. Covering: 70% viscose / 30% linen,
filling: synthetic beads, 38 × 54 cm
Vitra AG, Birsfelden, CH

Joris Laarman, Heatwave, 2003
Electronic radiator. Concrete,
aluminum, water, 65 × 250 × 45 cm
Jaga, Hasselt, BE

Patricia Urquiola, Antibodi, 2006
Couch. Leather, fabric,
stainless steel, 149 × 88 × 82 cm
Moroso Spa, Udine, IT

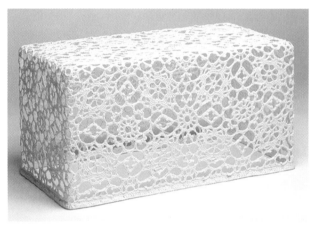

Marcel Wanders, Crochet, 2001
Side table. Cotton, epoxy, 60 × 30 × 30 cm
Moooi B.V., Breda, NL. Museum für Gestaltung Zürich, Designsammlung

**Eero Saarinen, No. 151,
Pedestal, Tulip, 1956**
Swivel chair. Cast aluminum,
fiberglass, foam plastic cushion,
51 × 54 × 81 cm
Knoll International.
Vitra Design Museum,
Weil am Rhein, DE

Tord Boontje, Garland Light, 2004
Pendant lamp.
Photo-etched stainless steel, 160 cm
Artecnica Inc., Los Angeles, US. Museum für
Gestaltung Zürich, Designsammlung

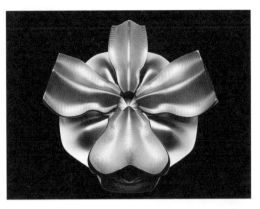

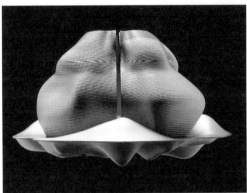

Greg Lynn, Alessi Tea & Coffee Towers, 2003
Double titanium wall, LYNCAF, coffeepot, 20 × 17.5 × 14.5 cm; LYNTEI, teapot, 20 × 17.5 × 16.5 cm; LYNCREM, milk ewer, 20 × 17.5 × 16.5 cm; LYNZUC, sugar dispenser, 20 × 12.5 × 16.5 cm; LYNVAS, tray, 8.5 × 44.5 × 44 cm
Alessi Spa, Crusinallo, IT

The Alessi Tea & Coffee Towers by Greg Lynn are part of a series for which Alessandro Mendini, commissioned by Alessi, invited important international architects to design. In Greg Lynn's contribution, the various elements are inspired in a flower and visible as a closed bud and also as open petals, revealing not only its forms but also its development process.

A design for cutlery, manufactured by Alessi as a prototype (see p. 162), takes up the structure of leaves and emphasizes the ribs of the venation system that supply the leaf with water and minerals and drain off the products of photosynthesis. Hence there are certain analogies to alimentation, in this case with the aid of cutlery inspired by the very processes of nature.

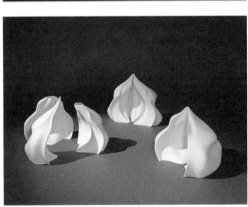

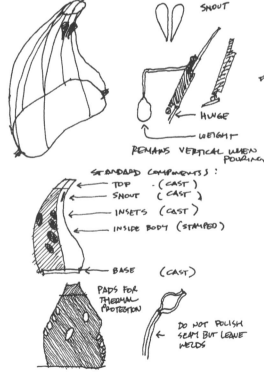

Greg Lynn, Alessi Cutlery, 2003
8 parts, prototypes, silver plated, 12–26 cm
Greg Lynn FORM, Los Angeles, US

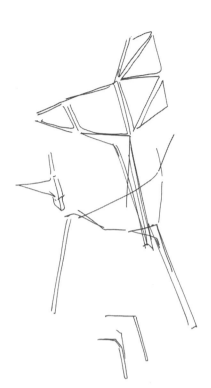

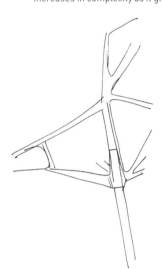

Konstantin Grcic, chair_ONE, stacking chair, 2004
Die-cast aluminum, 80 × 56 × 60 cm
Magis Spa, Motta di Livenza, IT

Depending on how one reads it, Konstantin Grcic's chair_ONE appears either as a crystalline structure or as a metaphor of a tree and its branch structure that increases in complexity as it grows.

Simon Heijdens, *Tree*, 2004
Interactive light installation with a tree and its leaves;
projectors; computer; wind, movement, and sound sensors;
size varies according to installation
Simon Heijdens, Rotterdam, NL

According to Simon Heijdens, nature has for the most
part vanished from the city, and even the trees on
the streets are more a part of urban design than natural
elements. There remain only a few phenomena,
such as wind, that are not influenced by this kind of
all-embracing design.

The interactive work *Tree* that has been shown at
various sites in Europe makes these phenomena visible
as the development process of an artificial nature.
An abstract outline of a tree measuring approximately

three by eight meters is projected onto various facades
in the city from sunset to sunrise. Its branches and
leaves move according to the intensity of the wind.
The leaves also react to movement and sounds. When
someone passes, or when a sound is made above
a certain noise level, a leaf falls from the tree; in the
course of the evening the tree grows increasingly bare.
The fallen leaf of light appears on the ground in a
nearby street, and the more leaves that fall from the
tree the brighter the location becomes. The increasing
density of the leaves is an indicator of the activity of
the city. But the light leaves also react to their surroundings—if one walks through them they roll to one side.

1930s–1970s

Taking off from Art Deco's crystalline structures, organic forms began to inspire design in the 1930s, reaching the apogee of its influence around the mid-twentieth century. As this formal idiom embellished the discontinuity and the raw quality of modernism, giving it a "natural" and familiar face, its projects seemingly always put forward the notion that natural forces could ultimately be tamed and, as it were, made useful.

The perspective on nature was transformed by images such as the photographs of the earth taken from Apollo 8 or the depiction of the double helix structure of DNA. Process and function became the central parameters of design, the possibility of manipulating nature moved to within grasping distance. In technoid futuristic visions mega-structures were developed that were oriented on the development of organisms.

**Alvar Aalto, Finnish Pavilion, World's Fair,
New York, US, 1938–39**

The Savoy Vase by Alvar Aalto from 1936 (see page 68) can certainly be described as *the* icon of organic design. In 1936, in the run-up to the Paris World's Fair, the Karhula Glassworks invited Alvar and Aino Aalto to participate in a competition that Alvar Aalto, who had already won the architecture competition for the Finnish Pavilion, clinched with his entry named *Eskimoerindens Skinnbuxa* (Eskimo Woman's Leather Pants). The so-called Aalto Vase was presented at the 1937 World's Fair in Paris, and in the same year its name was changed to Savoy Vase after

Aalto had chosen it for the interior of the restaurant of the same name in Helsinki. It is generally assumed that the curved form of the Savoy Vase is inspired by the Finnish coastlines, but these forms can just as well be related to anthropomorphic models or simply understood as an abstract expression of nature. An important aspect, and an indication of Aalto's overall concept, is that he also used these forms in his architecture, for example the pavilion for the New York World's Fair in 1939, which he transformed into an "organic exhibition."

**Friedrich Kiesler, view of the large model
for Endless House, New York 1959**
Cement, plaster, paint, wire netting, Plexiglas, 96.5 × 247 × 106.7 cm
Model owned by the Whitney Museum of American Art, New York, US.
Österreichische Friedrich und Lillian Kiesler-Privatstiftung

Endless House is a vision of the architect, designer, artist, and
stage designer Friedrich Kiesler, and is documented in numerous
models, drawings (see page 187), and writings. It is based on
the theory of Correalism, which "sees Man and his environment
as a holistic system of complex interactions." The biomorphic,
single-family house functions like an organism, combining all
areas of life in a bubble-shaped, integrated, individually-divisible
continuum. The elastic spatial concept can be appropriately
adapted to the requirements of its user.

R. Buckminster Fuller, Expo Dome, Expo 1967, Montreal, CA, 1965–67

Three-quarters of a geodesic dome constructed of a filigree two-layered, steel pipe, beam network, a transparent skin of acrylic panels with computer-controlled sun blinds. Height: 61 m, diameter: 76 m
Drawings of a segment of the dome and view of the dome

The US pavilion, backlit, from *Paris Match*, 1967

The American pavilion for Expo 67 in Montreal is Buckminster Fuller's most famous work and is emblematic for a design that understands itself as an anonymous, natural sphere. At first glance his designs do not contain natural forms, but deal with the relationship of systems, relative strengths, and the connection of people to their environment.

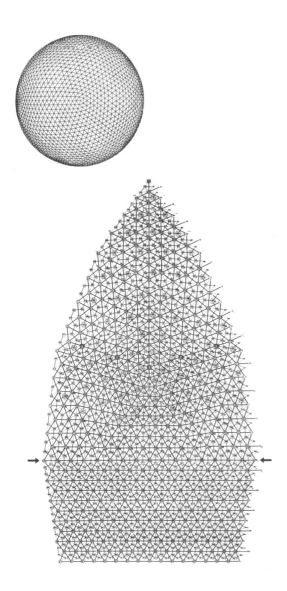

Behnisch & Partner, Frei Otto, Leonhardt & Andrä, roofing of the main sports facilities in the Olympiapark Munich, DE, 1967–72
Olympiagelände Munich, DE, 1972, view from the television tower of the swimming hall, the multi-purpose hall, the Olympiastadium, and, in the distance, the velodrome

Although Behnisch & Partner were the architects for the buildings constructed for the 1972 Olympic Games in Munich, the structural engineer Frei Otto, who repeatedly refers to the interactions between nature and technology in his work, and who had, together with Rolf Gutbrod, already caused a sensation with the roof construction for the German pavilion at Expo 67 in Montreal, was significantly involved in the roofing of the sports facilities. The innovative concept for the pavilion roof held by twelve steel pylons—whose cable-net construction is reminiscent of a system of interconnected spider webs—became an architectonic landmark of Munich and the expression of a lightness associated with nature in a conscious turning away from the 1936 Olympic Games organized by the Nazis.

Kiyonori Kikutake, Marine City, 1958
Drawing
Kiyonori Kikutake, architect, Tokyo, JP

In 1959, as the CIAM movement collapsed, Kisho
Kurokawa demanded a "shift from the age of machines
to the age of life." Alongside Kiyonori Kikutake, he
was one of the co-founders of the Metabolists group
formed in 1960. As a reaction to Japan's dense population
structure and the associated problems of overcrowded
cities, they designed megastructures capable of growth,
which could be modified and adapted to prevailing
requirements with plug-in units.

One of the most visionary designs is Kiyonori Kikutake's
Marine City from 1958. He designed an artificial industrial
city for Suruga Bay as a system of floating platforms
in the sea, intended to replace the traditional land-based
industrial complex. In 1961, Kisho Kurokawa developed
the Helix City project with a spiral structure oriented on
DNA. The three-dimensional cluster system was expandable
both vertically and horizontally. This idea for growth
oriented towards the development of organisms can also
be seen in his design for the Floating City of Kasumigaura,
the prototype of the Helix plan. However, here the
structure more closely resembles a branching plant stem
with blossoms forming at the ends of its shoots.

Kisho Kurokawa, Helix Sketch,
Project for a Helix City, Tokyo, JP, 1961
Kisho Kurokawa Architect & Associates, Tokyo, JP

Kisho Kurokawa, Kasumigaura Sketch,
Floating City project, Kasumigaura, Ibaraki, JP, 1961
Kisho Kurokawa Architect & Associates, Tokyo, JP

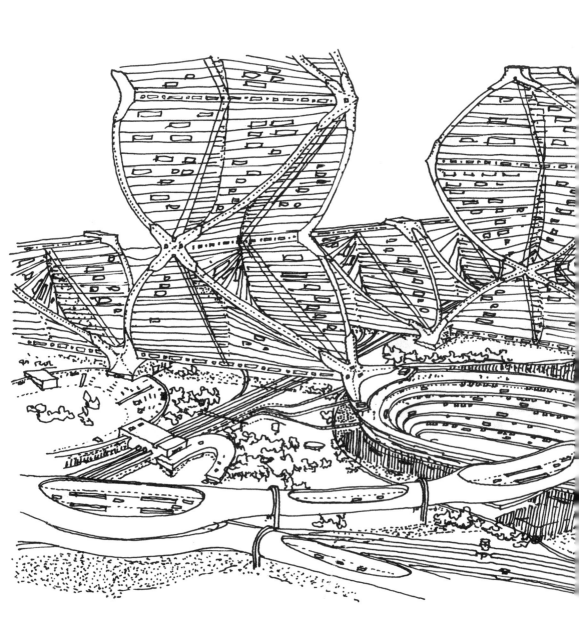

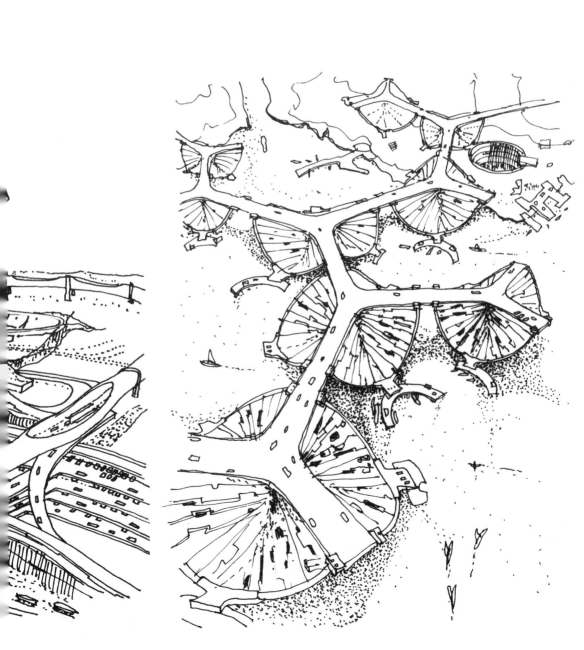

DOUBLE HELIX AND BLUE PLANET: THE VISUALIZATION OF NATURE IN THE TWENTIETH CENTURY

Philip Ursprung

The meaning of the term *nature* has changed radically in the course of the twentieth century. Rapid social, political, technical, and economic development; mechanized war; and the realization that man now has at his disposal the means to destroy the world through weapons of mass destruction have demolished the vision of nature as something self-evident, given, coherent, and inexhaustible. For many observers *nature* is only conceivable in quotation marks or, as the American artist Robert Smithson put it at the end of the 1960s, as "simply another eighteenth- and nineteenth-century fiction."[1] If nature is understood as a fiction—whether as a wish for continuity and coherence or as the notion that there exists an entirely different other—then the question about how nature influences design, in other words the way man is shaping his environment, must also be rephrased. If nature is not something given from inception, but a product or indeed a projection of mankind—that is, something first engendered by industrialization—then it can also be understood as design. That nature can be represented, that it can be depicted in the form of an image, text, or system of symbols, also harbors the possibility that it can be changed and manipulated. Seen from this perspective, nature and design shape each other.

The history during the period from the 1920s to the early 1970s of *nature design*—the term chosen as the title of this exhibition—can be presented in two distinct ways. On the one hand it can be presented as a continuation of late-nineteenth-century design, that is of a design that imitated or transformed specific forms of nature or natural forces. The predominant figures of this tradition were Alvar Aalto, Eero Saarinen, and Henry Moore. They oriented their work on organic forms in the broadest meaning of the term, and the way in which they used materials—whether it be wood, bronze, or concrete—reflected natural forces

1 Eero Saarinen, TWA Flight Center, Idlewild/ JFK Airport, New York, 1962
2 Alvar Aalto, United Nations General Assembly, New York, 1948–52

such as gravity, tectonics, erosion, etc., which are manifested through those very materials. Their approach is ultimately anti-modern and comparable with that of Antoni Gaudí, Emile Gallé, or Hector Guimard towards the end of the nineteenth century, as they sought their references in those forms displaced by industrialization. Their vocabulary of forms was universally understandable, particularly after the mid-twentieth century, and was successful and popular not only among specialists but also among politicians and businessmen. One reason for this was their development of a language that countered the discontinuity and rawness of modernism and gave it, as it were, a "natural" and familiar face. Another reason was that their projects centered on the theme that the forces of nature could be subjugated and ultimately benefited from.

Saarinen's iconic architecture—the former TWA Flight Center at John F. Kennedy Airport reminiscent of a bird spreading its wings in flight, the Ingalls Rink in New Haven known as "The Yale Whale," or the Gateway Arch in St. Louis—can be immediately understood by a broad public. By evoking natural models, a monumental, identity-establishing architecture is created (fig. 1). To a considerable extent, Aalto's architectural projects were so successful internationally because, independent of their size that ranged from a flower vase to a wooden chair, a student residence to the plenary hall of the United Nations, they seemed anthropomorphic and capable of integrating a human scale into even the most abstract political configurations (fig. 2). Finally, the large curving forms of Henry Moore's sculptures, with their suggestion of mater-

3 Henry Moore, *Reclining Figure*, 1953/54, bronze, length: 213 cm

nal protection were so effective as adornment for public buildings in Europe in the sixties and seventies because they perfectly reflected the vision of the post-war welfare state and its aim of planning for and guaranteeing the lives of its citizens **(fig. 3)**. Alongside Aalto, Saarinen, and Moore, designers and artists such as Arne Jacobsen, Isamu Noguchi, Charles and Ray Eames, and Joan Miró also belong to this formal tradition whose influence can still be felt today.

While this branch of tradition is based on the premise that nature and design are complementary to each other, and that design can reflect and imitate nature, the other branch is based on the premise that the concepts of nature and design are not separate but rather inseparably interwoven. This understanding of nature design assumes that during the course of the 1930s, nature could no longer be adequately represented as an image, or a form, for example in guise of floral motifs or the evocation of natural forces. It assumes that the iconographical reservoir had been exhausted some time at the beginning of the 1930s, and that nature had, so to speak, become invisible. And it also assumes that figures such as Aalto, Saarinen, and Moore, though highly successful in their time, did not represent a new tradition as their vocabularies referenced the past.

From this perspective, nature is just as designed as design is natural; life is planned in the same way that the plan is something alive. The assumption that nature and design cannot be separated from each other offers the possibility of rephrasing the question about the very relationship between nature and design. In this context, design is not under-

4 James D. Watson and Francis Crick in front of the DNA model, 1953
5 Cover of *The Double Helix* by James D. Watson, New York, 1968

stood as product design—thus making it a sub-category ascribed by Modernism to a lower order within the visual culture than art and architecture—but in a far broader way as design, planning, visualization of politics, business, environment, the future, indeed of human life in general. The term *nature design* therefore encompasses a series of practices that intervene directly in the control and shaping of human life, such as genetic engineering, climate control, birth control, the organization of states, the distribution of risk in insurance and pension plans, as well as politicians' election strategies and the advertising campaigns of fashion concerns.

DOUBLE HELIX AND THE RISING OF THE MOON

The depiction of the structure of genetic material by the American biologist James Watson and the English physicist Francis Crick in Cambridge in 1953 represented a decisive step in the history of the relationship between nature and design. They depicted the structure of DNA in the form of a double helix. The two-meter-high model became a new emblem of nature (fig. 4). It was a spatial representation that not only allowed us to understand the mechanisms of heredity transmission, but also offered the basis for manipulating them—a potential that both researchers pointed out in their publication in the magazine *Nature* in 1953: "It has not escaped our notice that the specific pairing we have postulated immediately suggests a possible copying mechanism for the genetic material."[2] The effect on the public caused by the image of

6 The blue planet against a black universe, NASA 1968, *Life*, January 1969

the double helix actually took place much later, fifteen years after its discovery and five years after the awarding of the Nobel Prize to Watson and Crick. In 1968, the publication of James Watson's bestseller *The Double Helix* made this geometric figure into an icon for nature (fig. 5). The message was clear: nature was no longer the mysterious other we are at the mercy of, but had become a language that we could master. With the "decoding" of the genetic code, as it was called in the 1950s language of the Cold War, the creation of a "Library of Life," as it was to be called in the language of Empire at the turn of the millennium, had become possible.

The triumph of the double helix coincided with another influential image of nature: the photographs by NASA of the planet Earth. The circulation of the pictures from Apollo 8 showing the blue planet against a black universe, or the earth rising above the surface of the moon, shaped

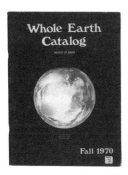

7 *Whole Earth Catalog*, 1970

an entire generation's concept of nature (fig. 6). Nature was visualized in an immeasurably enlarged and an immeasurably reduced way; on the one hand as a system of molecular building blocks, on the other as a vulnerable, self-contained system subjected to an immense nothingness. The term nature was thus replaced by the conception of systems and balances of forces of which man formed a part, but the future of which he could also help to shape. This change of scale led to the product becoming less important than the process, the form less important than the function.

Typical of the changing design of this time were projects like the *Whole Earth Catalog* produced between 1969 and the early 1970s, an encyclopedic collection of objects or, as they were called, tools, which would permit us to better shape the human environment, to protect limited resources, and to develop alternatives to the established forms of industrialized society (fig. 7). The *Whole Earth Catalog* and the environmental protection movement that took off at around the same time—particularly in 1971 with the NGO Greenpeace—aimed at protecting the fragile "System Earth" and shaping a new lifestyle. Paradoxically, others with completely different motives also succeeded in operating under the canopy of this new understanding of nature. The drastic increase in oil prices that international energy companies and OPEC imposed on consumers of the industrialized nations in the seventies—the beginning of what has been known since the nineties as globalization—was not interpreted by the general public as the result of merciless exploitation and cynical calculation on the part of cartels, but as a "natural" prob-

8 Richard Buckminster Fuller, Expo-Dome, American Pavilion for Expo 67 in Montreal
9 Frei Otto, Olympic Stadium Munich, 1967–72

lem—the consequence of limited oil resources.[3] The image of the tiny blue planet was so strongly anchored in people's minds that consumers were ready to accept the arbitrary price hikes and the economic recession that followed as a natural phenomenon rather than to fight it as a political and economic decision. And in the seventies, genuinely global companies such as IKEA or Benetton began not only to supply the international middle classes with reasonably priced furniture and clothing of decent quality, but to shape an international lifestyle that suggested a local identity and that embodied "naturalness."

THE LARGE WHOLE

As the process grew to be more important than the product, the system more important than the form, and the event more important than the object, traditional professional boundaries became increasingly blurred. The key historical figure in nature design during the period from the 1930s to the 1970s was Richard Buckminster Fuller. Given the multi-faceted nature of his practice, the definitions of architecture, art, design, theory, and fiction began to topple. In the twenties, Fuller started to develop new technical visions. His success is inseparably linked to the U.S. military industry, for which in the forties and fifties he developed processes for mobile architectures that functioned like systems. His concepts for self-supporting systems—such as the tensegrity system— were used for military structures, such as protective coverings for radar antennae, but soon found use in exhibition architecture and mobile

10 Friedrich Kiesler, *Study for the Endless House*, 1960. Pencil on tracing paper, 20 × 29.7 cm
Österreichische Friedrich und Lillian Kiesler-Privatstiftung

forms of housing that interested, for example, readers of the *Whole Earth Catalog*. Buckminster Fuller's saying, "think global, act local," became the slogan of a movement that remained conscious of its responsibility for the entire "System Earth"—and was later instrumentalized by globalized business. Fuller's best-known work, the American Pavilion for the Expo 67 in Montreal, is emblematic as a design that sees itself as an autonomous natural sphere. This object continues to attract visitors today under the name Biosphère (fig. 8).

While at first glance Fuller's design may not seem based on natural forms, in fact his designs all deal with systematic contexts, the balance of forces, and the connection of man to his environment. The work of German architect Frei Otto, who became known for his space-frame structures in the fifties, is comparable. Although in later publications Frei Otto explicitly refers to his inspiration in natural forms,[4] projects such as his signature work, the 1972 Munich Olympic Stadium, are, like those of Buckminster Fuller, self-contained entities based on modular systems in which the smallest detail corresponds with the whole (fig. 9).

While Fuller and Frei Otto were mainly influential on engineers and until recently remained outside the canon of art and architectural history, Friedrich Kiesler has since the fifties been an integrative figure who made his mark both on exhibition design and the visual arts and architecture. His Endless House (fig. 10) is conceived entirely from the interior spaces, and deals with how interflowing spatial shells can surround the users without subjecting them to arbitrary systems or aesthetic conventions. For artists of the late fifties such as Robert Rauschenberg,

Allan Kaprow, or Claes Oldenburg, Kiesler proved to be so inspirational because he articulated environments that surrounded people with specific material and atmospheric situations, and provided them the opportunity to influence these environments.

Though the protagonists of nature design such as Fuller or Kiesler became active in the thirties, only in the fifties did their influence begin to be felt. If the consciousness of nature's vulnerability that developed around 1970 created a public sensitivity to images such as those of the double helix and the planet Earth, the question arises as to why nature lost visibility in the 1930s. Why was nature suddenly no longer perceived as a form but as a system? Why in the thirties—described as a phase of *rappel à l'ordre*—are there so many attempts to fix an environment perceived as chaotic in clearly defined forms within the framework of the visual culture? The obsession of artists, architects, and designers with monumental forms is a symptom of the old order's disintegration in the hands of contemporaries. This change is clearly revealed in the conspicuous preference at the time for crystalline structures. From the surfaces of skyscraper façades to the glittering inclusions in the stones of the Chrysler Building lobby in New York, or to the surface of tortoise shell etuis and indeed in the musical structure of jazz, there was a definite preference for crystalline structures (fig. 11). It is an emphasis on the discontinuity and internal contradiction, an alternative image to the soft organic forms that had dominated the visual culture of the preceding decades—and at the same time a reference to the molecular forces that also occur in nature. If the hypothesis is true that the economic transformation of the late sixties and early seventies was the cause of the new perception of nature, then the destruction of the earlier image of nature could have been due to the economic crisis in 1929. For in contrast to the triumph of capitalism—the start of globalization in the early seventies—of which the most striking image is paradoxically that of the "oil crisis," no image represents the total collapse of the economic system more faithfully than that of the Great Crash of 1929. At the time capitalism suffered a defeat that, ever since, it has attempted to prevent a repetition of at any cost. In the loss of control over market forces, its nature could, for a brief moment, be clearly seen: a scandalous, immensely aggressive nature, infinitely more threatening than all the storms, volcanic eruptions, and ocean tempests together.

11 William van Alen, Chrysler Building, New York, 1928–30

It was clear that market forces could never again be left uncontrolled. In the future they had to be controlled and designed. It is this nature—which in modernism can have no image—that must remain suppressed. The history of nature design is a function of economic history.

1 Robert Smithson, "A Museum of Language in the Vicinity of Art", *Art International,* March 1968; reprinted in *Robert Smithson: The Collected Writings,* ed. Jack Flam, Berkeley, 1996, p. 85.
2 J.D. Watson and F.H.C. Crick, "A Structure for Deoxyribose Nucleic Acid", *Nature* 171 (April 25, 1953), pp. 737–38.

3 For a critical portrayal of the energy crisis see: The Midnight Notes Collective, ed., *Midnight Oil: Work, Energy, War, 1972–93,* San Francisco, 1992.
4 Frei Otto, *Gestaltwerdung, zur Formentstehung in Natur, Technik und Baukunst,* Cologne, 1988.

OMORPHE

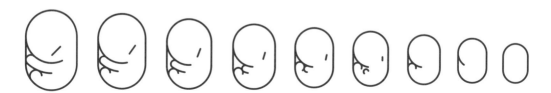

**Design Square One SRL, Embryo Nightclub,
Bucharest, RO, 2006**

The four-part logo of this new nightclub in Bucharest refers
to the organic theme that inspired its design: the various
stages of development of an embryo. The entrance
area leading into the windowless ground and basement
floors is like a vagina; in the underbelly of the club a three-
dimensional wall made of Comadur panels in the form
of an oversized cell structure encloses the space. Comple-
menting this variably colored, womb-like space, the
rest of the interior fittings and the light membrane also
imitate organic forms. The procreative process is also
represented in the indirect lighting slots in the bar area,
which are in the form of sperm cells.

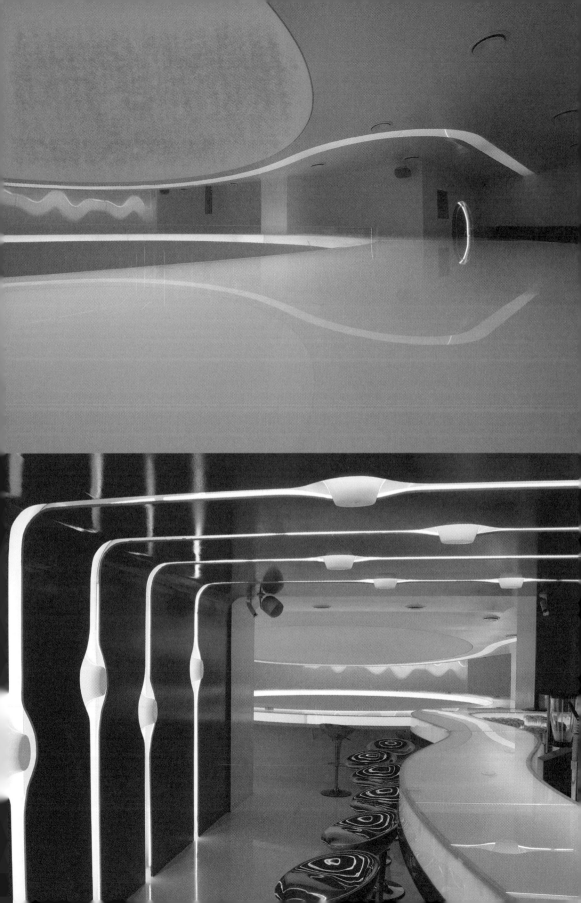

Herzog & de Meuron, Jingzi, 2005
Lamp. Silicone: 45 × 30 cm, tubular cable: 155–166.5 cm
Belux AG, Wohlen, CH. Property of the Swiss Confederation,
Federal Office of Culture Bern, on permanent loan to
the Designsammlung of the Museum für Gestaltung Zürich

Marc Newson, Embryo Chair, 1988
Tubular steel, polyurethane, neoprene, 80 × 85 × 80 cm
Cappellini, Arosio, IT

Gaetano Pesce, La Mamma, 1969
Chair. Structure: Bayfit® (Bayer®) flexible cold-
shaped polyurethane foam, cover: jersey, base: jute,
chair: 103 × 120 × 130 cm, pouf: 57 cm
B&B Italia Spa, Noverate, IT

**Alessandro Mendini,
Anna G. Corkscrew, 1994**
Stainless steel, plastic, 24.5 × 7 cm
Alessi Spa, Crusinallo, IT

Kurt Thut, Kleiderständer Nr. 107, 1998
Garment rack. Varnished beech,
131 × 60 × 35 cm (variable)
Thut Möbel, Möriken, CH. Property of the Swiss
Confederation, Federal Office of Culture Bern,
on permanent loan to the Designsammlung of the
Museum für Gestaltung Zürich

Anonymous, Kidney-shaped table, Switzerland, ca. 1950s
Frame: wood, with three wooden legs, tabletop covered
with black synthetic leather, 85 × 55 × 52.5 cm
Museum für Gestaltung Zürich, Designsammlung

Richard Hutten, Dombo, 2002
Child's cup. Plastic, 9 × 26 cm
Richard Hutten Collection B.V., Rotterdam, NL

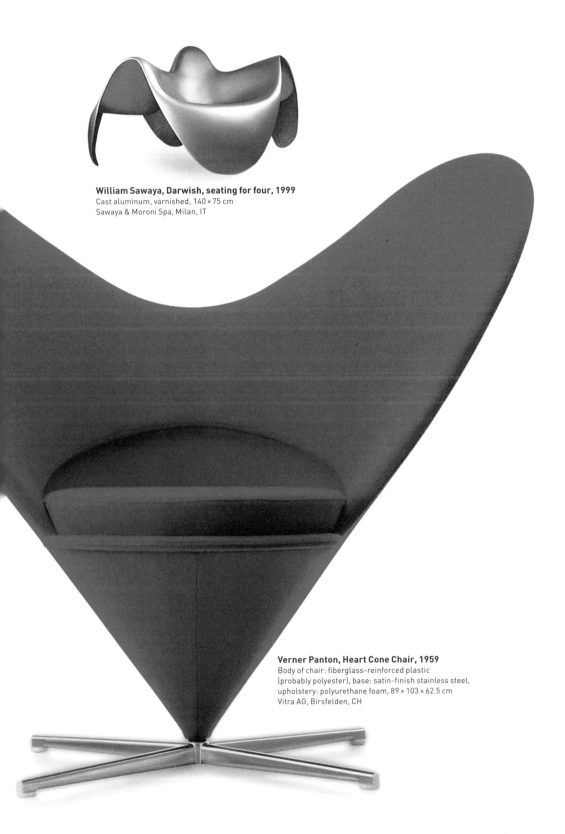

William Sawaya, Darwish, seating for four, 1999
Cast aluminum, varnished, 140 × 75 cm
Sawaya & Moroni Spa, Milan, IT

Verner Panton, Heart Cone Chair, 1959
Body of chair: fiberglass-reinforced plastic
(probably polyester), base: satin-finish stainless steel,
upholstery: polyurethane foam, 89 × 103 × 62.5 cm
Vitra AG, Birsfelden, CH

Aino and Alvar Aalto, Model 31, 1932
Cantilevered armchair. Frame: bent and molded
laminated birch, seat: molded plywood, 60 × 60 × 60 cm
O.y. Huonekalu – ja Rakennustyötehdas A.b., Turku, FI
Museum für Gestaltung Zürich, Designsammlung

Arne Jacobsen, Model 3117, 1955
Office chair with castors. Chrome-plated steel tubing,
bent plywood, varnished oak veneer, plastic, 82 × 48.5 × 48 cm
Fritz Hansen Eft. A/S, Allerod, DK
Museum für Gestaltung Zürich, Designsammlung

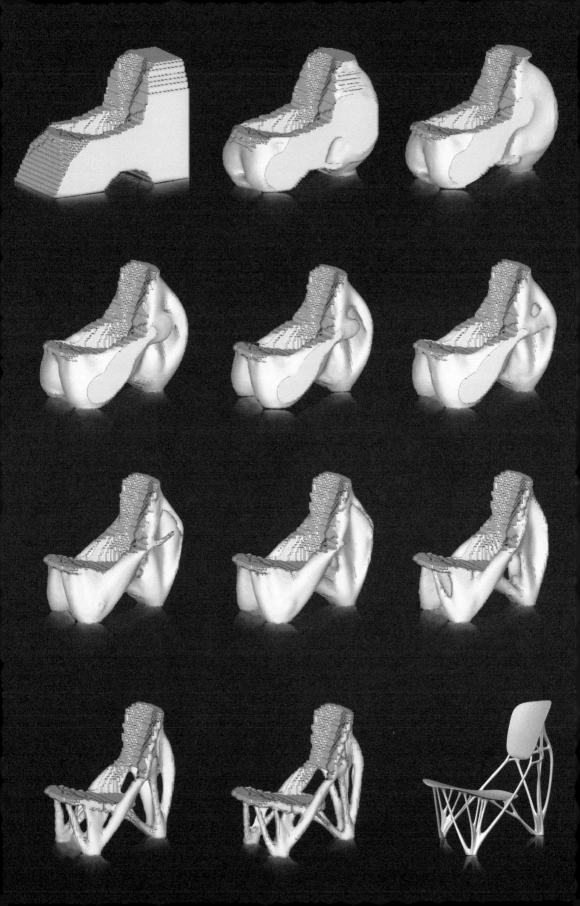

Joris Laarman, Bone Chair, 2007
Polished aluminum, 75.6 × 44.5 × 76.8 cm
Gallery Barry Friedman Ltd, New York, US, & droog, Amsterdam, NL

If the evolutionary process could create a chair [...] is the
motto of this piece of seating sculpture. The construction
starts from the premise that trees are capable of adding
material at the points where a particular degree of stability
is required, and bones are able to reduce the amount
of material where it is not needed. With this knowledge the
International Development Centre Adam Opel AG, which
is part of General Motors Engineering Europe, developed
a dynamic digital tool that imitates these processes to
yield optimized car parts. It is a copy of the method by which
structures in nature evolve. Joris Laarman used this tool
to develop a chair in the form of a dynamic skeleton. It forms
part of both a (design) process and a series, in which the
laws of construction can be applied on different scales
in accordance with the respective material, and be extended
up to an architecture scale.

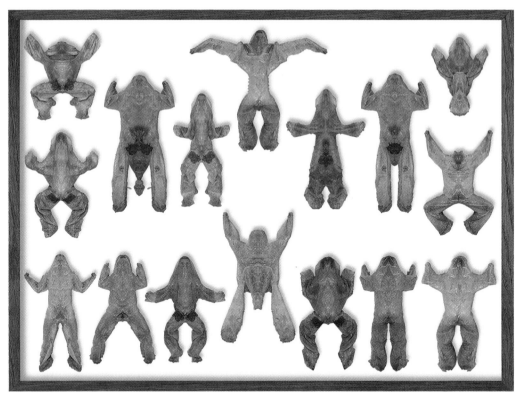

Olivier Goulet, *Boîte d'insectes anthropomorphes n° 2,* **1998**
Cibachrome, 30 × 40 cm
Olivier Goulet, Paris, FR

Olivier Goulet, *Twin,* **2001**
Latex, 20 × 9, 2 × 60, 25 × 13 cm
Olivier Goulet, Paris, FR

Olivier Goulet, *Combinaison,* **2004**
Latex, life-size
Olivier Goulet, Paris, FR

Olivier Goulet's skin objects, whether they are body
suits or bags formed like human organs made of latex,
are conceived as an extension of the human body,
as the shedding of a skin at the interface between the
individual and the environment. The box with the anthropomorphic insects evokes zoological displays of collections
of butterflies (see pp. 28/29) or beetles, mounted on
pins and arranged to convey a systemic depiction of the
various species.

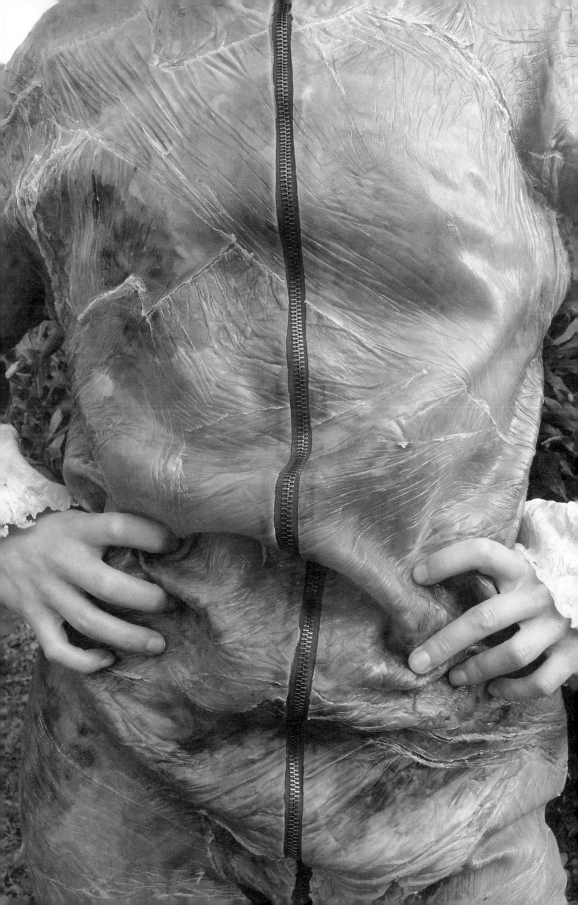

OMORPHE

**Werner Aisslinger, mesh – modular knitting structure,
for the exhibition *Nature Design*,
Museum für Gestaltung Zürich, 2007**
Modules made of synthetic fibers by a 3D knitted web technique
with adhesive heat distortion, module: 40 × 40 × 8 cm
Werner Aisslinger, Berlin, DE.
Engineering: Visiotex, Neu-Ulm, DE

The mesh-honeycomb project forms organic spaces that do
not consist of solid structures, but with gaps, compressions,
and overlays are woven together like a canopy of leaves.
The three types of light honeycomb modules are knitted in
a high-tech process, warped three-dimensionally by heat,
and then stiffened. They can be added to infinitely, and linked
to form walls, spatial shells, screens, or tunnels. Different
colors of woven fibers and changing weave directions
create perforated and compressed surface textures. The
translucent and osmotic module structures can subdivide
open architectures or create sub-spaces without screening
them off entirely from view. On the one hand, its structure
evokes that of insects' constructions; on the other, the
addition of elements creates organic, tree-like structures
that recall an extreme close-up of a leaf.

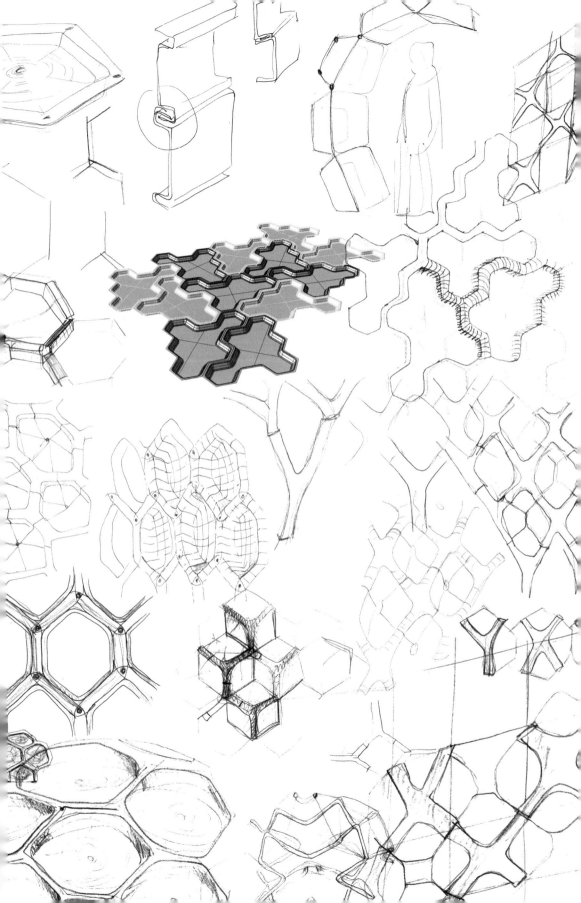

**Arne Jacobsen,
The Ant chair, 1952**
Wood, metal, 78 × 44 × 40 cm
Fritz Hansen Eft. A/S, Allerod, DK
Museum für Gestaltung Zürich,
Designsammlung

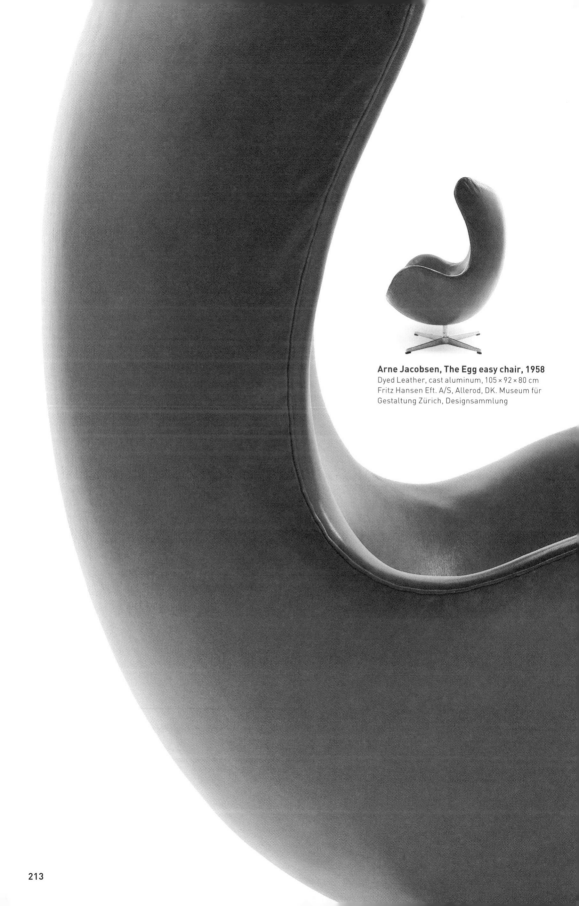

Arne Jacobsen, The Egg easy chair, 1958
Dyed Leather, cast aluminum, 105 × 92 × 80 cm
Fritz Hansen Eft. A/S, Allerod, DK. Museum für
Gestaltung Zürich, Designsammlung

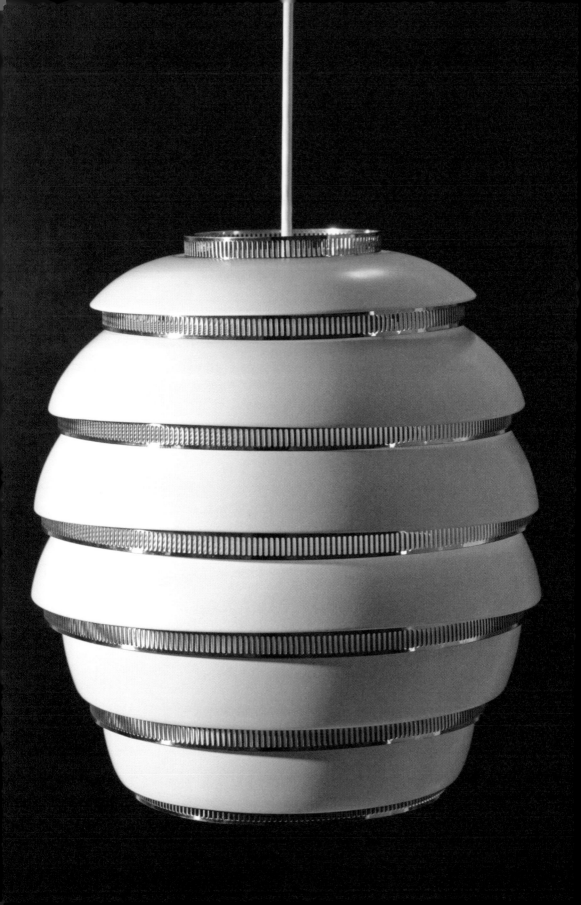

Alvar Aalto, A 331, "Beehive," 1953
Pendant lamp. Layers of painted matte steel
and brass, 30 × 33 cm
Vitra Design Museum, Weil am Rhein, DE

Ron Arad, Bookworm Bookcase, 1993
Batch-dyed thermoplastic, 19 × 520 × 20 cm
Kartell Spa, Milan, IT

Ettore Cimini, Rā, 2002
Table lamp. Metal and technopolymer, two
independently adjustable arms, light is transmitted
through silicon fiber optics, ca. 100 × 26 cm
Lumina (Schweiz) GmbH, Langendorf, CH

Ferdinand Porsche, Volkswagen, 1938–2003
Beetle. Automobile
Volkswagen AG, Wolfsburg, DE

**Grupo Austral, Jorge Ferrari-Hardoy,
Butterfly chair (Hardoy chair,
BKR chair), 1938, here 1950s**
Light brown suede,
black metal frame, 80 × 88 × 90 cm
Knoll International. Reinhart Hoffmeister,
Munich, DE

Sori Yanagi, Butterfly Stool, 1954
Lacquered bent plywood, brass fittings,
39 × 42 × 31 cm
Vitra AG, Birsfelden, CH

**Christoph Dietlicher,
Thomas Drack, Andreas
Giupponi, Pinguin, 1989**
Table lamp. Sheet steel,
powder-coated, 51 × 34 × 35 cm
Neue Werkstatt, Winterthur, CH.
Museum für Gestaltung Zürich,
Designsammlung

Karim Rashid, KenzoAmour, 2006
Three perfume bottles. Glass, high-density
polypropylene, varnish, 30 ml: 17 × 5.5 cm,
50 ml: 19.5 × 6 cm, 100 ml: 21 × 6.5 cm
Kenzo Parfums, Paris, FR

Ingo Maurer, Lucellino, 1992
Table lamp. Glass, brass, plastic, goose feathers, 25.4 × 20.3 × 10.8 cm
Ingo Maurer GmbH, Munich, DE. Museum für Gestaltung Zürich, Designsammlung

Ted Muehling, Eivase, 2000
Egg vase. Porcelain, 12 cm
Porzellan-Manufaktur Nymphenburg, Munich, DE

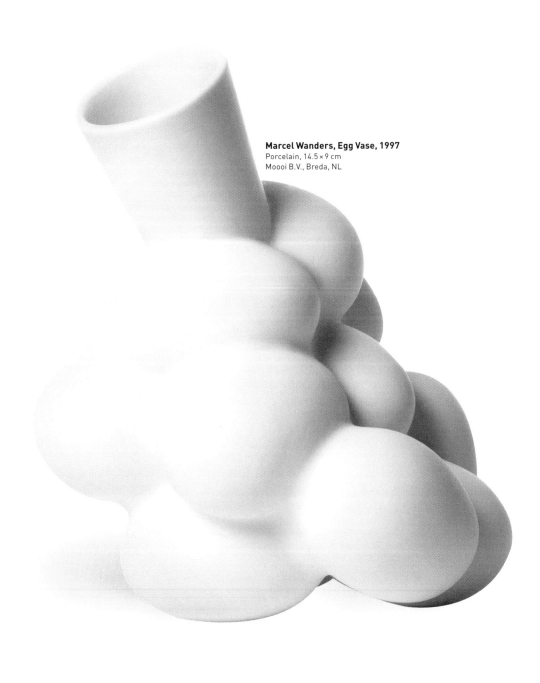

Marcel Wanders, Egg Vase, 1997
Porcelain, 14.5 × 9 cm
Moooi B.V., Breda, NL

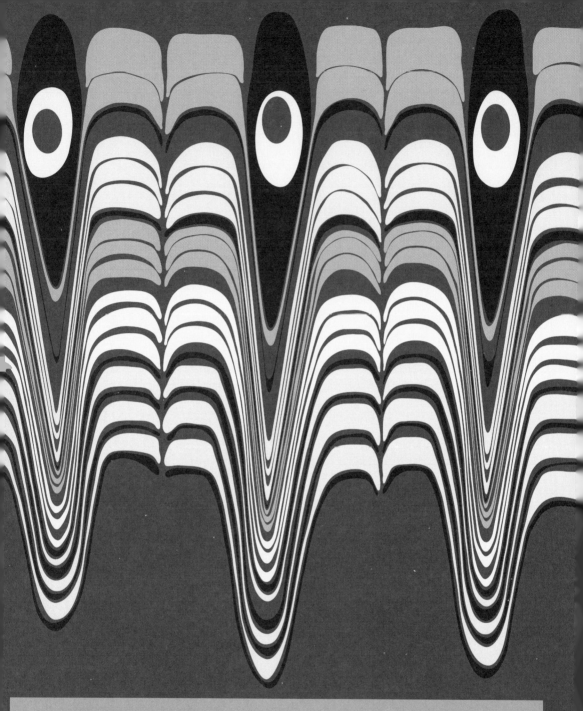

Olaf Nicolai, *Yeux de Paon*, 2007
Eye of the Peacock's Tail. Woven silk and cotton, 320 × 840 cm
Olaf Nicolai, Berlin, DE. Carolina Nitsch Contemporary Art, New York,
US. Courtesy Galerie EIGEN+ART, Leipzig / Berlin, DE

In works such as *Itamaraty* (1995), or the project
Interieur / Landschaft (1997) for the *documenta X* in Kassel,
Olaf Nicolai has repeatedly investigated and represented
the intersection of nature and the reaction to it, design,
and art. Behind a particular object there is always
concealed a complex history, a mesh of relationships
between the models, the objects, and their translation
into new objects.

The eye of the peacock's tail is certainly one of the more
striking patterns within nature, but in his long length
of fabric *Yeux de Paon* Olaf Nicolai alludes to its use as
ornament in Bulgarian ceramic work. With the use
of this traditional peasant motif in the tourist-fed mass
production of the 1970s, the symbol became a "synonym
for Bulgarian folklore." Consequently, the project
considers travel in its modern incarnation as tourism
of the masses, the construction of identity founded upon
an "authentic" souvenir, and attempts at historical
determinism. Olaf Nicolai establishes distance by de-
contextualizing the motif and showing it in non-colors.

Sony Corporation, Hajime Sorayama,
Aibo Entertainment Robot (ERS-110), 1999
Toy robot. Various materials, 26.7 × 15.2 × 41.3 cm
Sony Overseas SA, Schlieren, CH

Miriam van der Lubbe, Poodle chair, 2002
Two chairs, brown: groomed, white: un-groomed, each 40 × 80 × 80 cm
Miriam van der Lubbe, Geldrop, NL

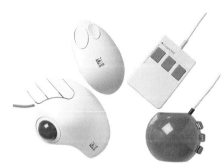

Logitech, Computer Mouses, n.d
Plastic
Logitech Europe SA, Romanel sur Morges, CH.
Museum für Gestaltung Zürich, Designsammlung

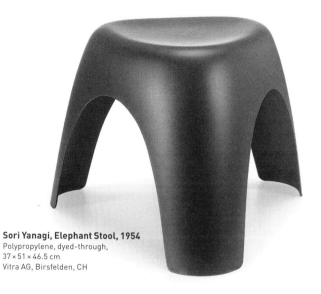

Sori Yanagi, Elephant Stool, 1954
Polypropylene, dyed-through,
37 × 51 × 46.5 cm
Vitra AG, Birsfelden, CH

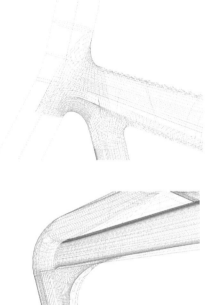

Konstantin Grcic, MIURA, Bar Stool, 2004
Reinforced polypropylene, 81 × 78 × 53 × 55 cm
Plank Collezioni Srl, Ora, IT

Wieki Somers, High Tea Pot, 2003
Bone China porcelain, fur (water rat), stainless steel,
leather, 47 × 20 × 25 cm
European Ceramic Work Centre EKWC, Den Bosch, NL

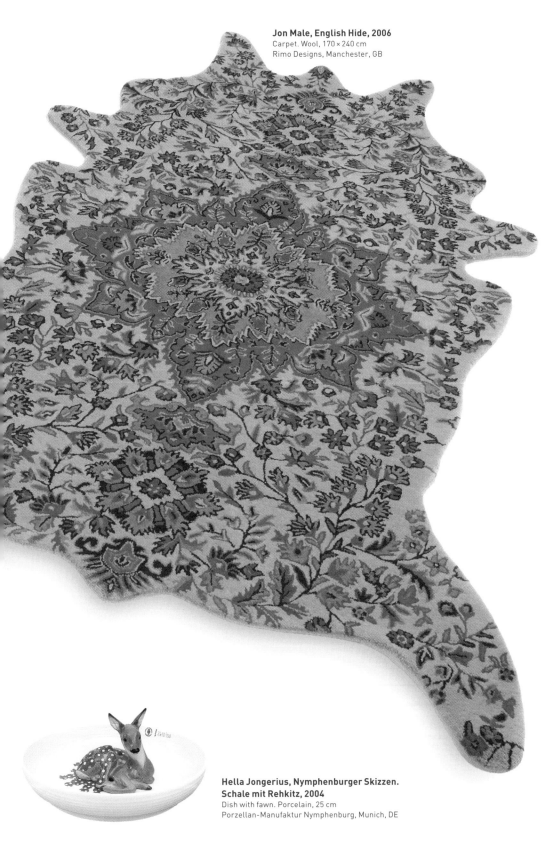

Jon Male, English Hide, 2006
Carpet. Wool, 170 × 240 cm
Rimo Designs, Manchester, GB

Hella Jongerius, Nymphenburger Skizzen.
Schale mit Rehkitz, 2004
Dish with fawn. Porcelain, 25 cm
Porzellan-Manufaktur Nymphenburg, Munich, DE

Jürgen Mayer H., Danfoss Universe, Extension (Phase II), Food Factory and Curiosity Center, Nordborg, DK, 2007
J. Mayer H., Berlin, DE

CONTEMPORARY

Since the 1990s there has been a notable renaissance in Nature Design, expressing itself in a wide range of forms and functions. Design oriented on nature seems to acquire relevance whenever modern society finds itself in crisis as it searches to re-establish a harmonious relationship with an environment perceived as out of balance or hostile.

The examination of nature is also playing an important and influential role in contemporary architecture with its theoretical complexities. In design we find work inspired by natural forms and processes, the fluid forms of Blob Design, and material research and bionics in which naturally occurring structures are made manifest through technological advancements. Biotechnology goes one step further and intervenes in the system of nature in order to change its very construction—an experiment with an uncertain outcome.

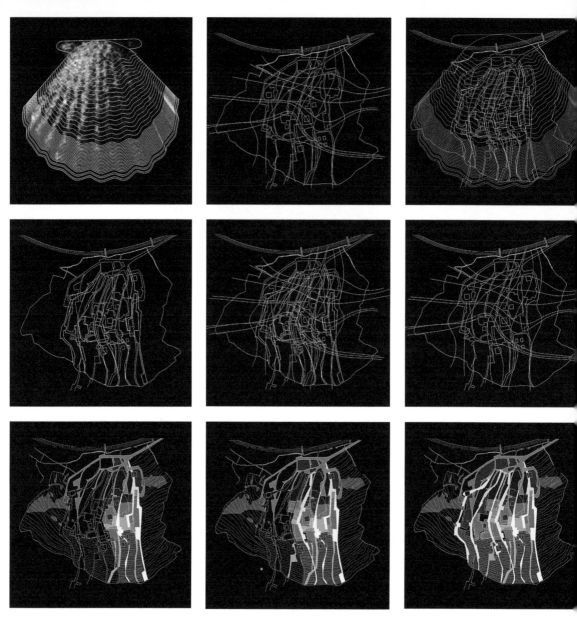

**Peter Eisenman, City of Culture of Galicia,
Santiago de Compostela, ES, since 1999**
Eisenman Architects, New York, US
Diagram with the evolution of the layout, including
the traditional symbol of Santiago—the St. James's shell
....
Series of diagrams with the three-dimensional
forming of the layered site plan
....
pp. 232/233
Competition model, 1999
....
Aerial photograph from the southeast, buildings from
foreground to background: Hemeroteca (Periodicals Archive),
Library, Museum of Galician History
....
Layout
....
Aerial view, clockwise from top left: Museum of Galician History,
Central Services building, Library, Hemeroteca

For the development of the City of Culture of Galicia,
Peter Eisenman uses the strategy of encoding with which,
as with DNA code, it is possible to re-order a given context.
At the beginning, a series of plans are laid over each
other—the medieval street pattern in the form of St. James's
Shell, the symbol of Santiago de Compostela; the abstract
Cartesian coordinates system with its mathematical
rationalism; and the topological surface of the site—these
overlaid plans are then transcribed into a three-dimensional
vector matrix.

Nature becomes visible here in the basic underlying
form of St. James's shell and the topography, but also in the
concept of DNA, the carrier of genetic make-up, which is
an apposite paraphrase of Eisenman's concept of a physical
and cultural archaeology from which contemporary
architecture emerges.

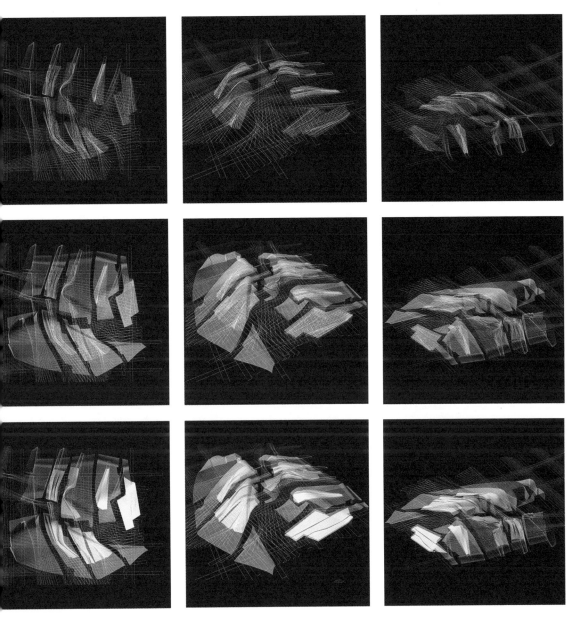

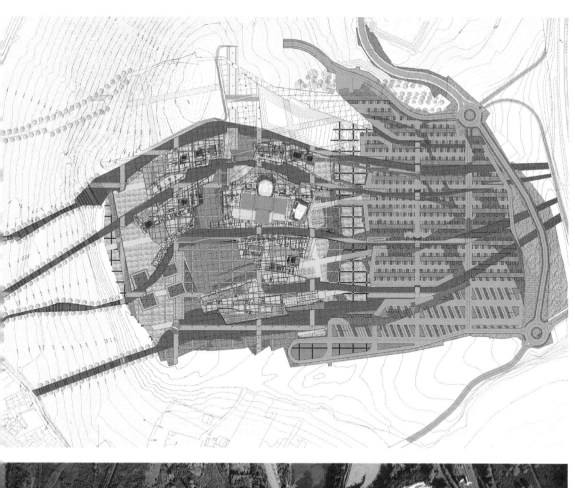

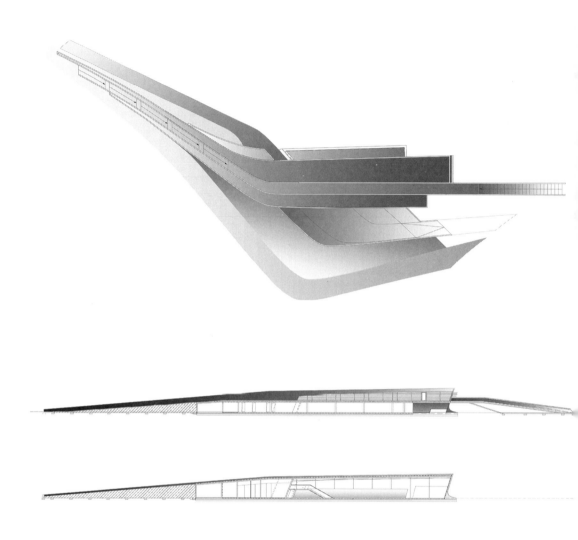

Zaha Hadid, LFOne / Landesgartenschau,
Weil am Rhein, DE, 1996–99
Zaha Hadid Architects, London, GB
pp. 234/235: Details and view

Roof view, longitudinal sections

Detail views

With the exhibition rooms, a restaurant, and offices in
the pavilion for the Landesgartenschau in Weil am Rhein,
Zaha Hadid uses the topography as a reference, as she
does with her Z-Scape furniture (see page 114). The flowing
spaces relate to "natural landscape formations such as
estuaries, mountain chains, forests, deserts, gorges, floating
ice fields, and seas." Correspondingly, the four parallel
partly-interwoven and overlapping spatial structures do
not assert themselves as an isolated object, but emerge from
the surroundings and appear to flow into it.

Zaha Hadid, extension of the Ordrupgaard Museum, Copenhagen, DK, 2001–05
Zaha Hadid Architects, London, GB
Layout
Views

The extension of the Ordrupgaard Museum offered the opportunity to create new formal relationships between the museum buildings and the surrounding garden. The ensemble, with its outer walls swinging up out of the ground and merging into the roof, with its external form and the interior spatial landscapes, becomes topography itself, a new landscape within the given surroundings with which it enters into fluid interaction. This concept is reinforced by means of the camouflage in the opaque concrete walls and the transparency of the spacious glassed areas that reflect the landscape, and permit interior and exterior views.

**R&Sie(n), Green Gorgon (Project),
Lausanne, CH, 2005**
R&Sie(n), Paris, FR
Bird's eye view
....
Page 242/243
Inspirations
....
Panorama

The competition design for a museum on the shore of Lake
Geneva in Lausanne combines the aura of a biotope with
the concept of a labyrinth, intended to be reminiscent of the
diversity of the collections. Entangled structures reflect in
the water, evoking both Ophelia's hair and Mucha's lithographs
(see page 97), and, according to R&Sie(n), conjuring up a
place out of a Grimm fairytale in which fascination and fear
merge in the middle of a forest. The wild, vegetable, urban, and
artificial components of nature meet here to form a building
that is in turn landscape itself. This is also expressed in its green
mantle, a kind of biodynamic skin capable of filtering dust
and purifying the atmosphere.

Onodrims, "figure" de la forêt

Une ambassade de la compagnie des indes (Jan Nieuhof / 1669)

Labyrinthe avec cabinets et fontaine

Insecte brance "Phasme"

Lianes spontanées

Va

(Dézallier d'Argenville)

La maison de la veuve Winchester

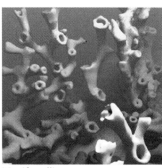

Massif corallien

Vicomte (Le Nôtre)

Murs végétaux sur support artificiel

Toyo Ito, Sendai Mediatheque,
Sendai-shi, Miyaki, JP, 1995–2001
Toyo Ito & Associates, Architects, Tokyo, JP
Interior view of one floor
....
Draft sketch
....
Tube plate skin diagram
....
Partial view of the building

The Sendai Mediatheque is a multi-functional cultural center
containing a multimedia library, a film studio, and a café.
The specifications of this project and its function within the
city led Ito to design a building that is as open and transparent as possible, whose main elements are the supports on
the extremely minimized floor plates of the freely divisible
floors and the transparent façade. Ito took inspiration from
seaweed floating in water for the thirteen lattice-shaped,
painted-steel supporting columns, which could also be interpreted as a tree structure. The tubes that shoot upwards
through seven floors have varying diameters and continually
change direction; on the one hand, providing the statics
of the building, and on the other accommodating the whole
supply and infrastructure facilities required by the multimedia center. They are the element that, alongside the activity
within, bestows life and radiance upon the building.

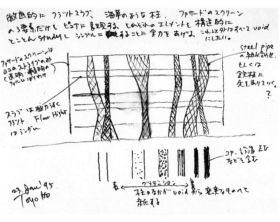

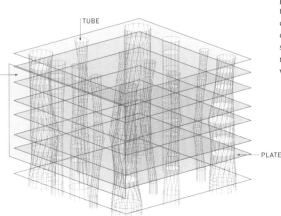

Herzog & de Meuron, Auditorium du Jura, Courgenay, CH, project 2005–06
Herzog & de Meuron, Basel, CH. Client:
Fondation de l'Auditorium du Jura, Porrentruy, CH
Landscape view

The Auditorium du Jura dates back to an initiative of Georges and Rémy Zaugg, and is itself paying homage to the artist Rémy Zaugg who frequently worked with Herzog & de Meuron. He also devised the concept of a cultural triangle between Courgenay, Ronchamp (site of Le Corbusier's Notre-Dame-du-Haut pilgrimage chapel), and Ornans (birthplace of Gustave Courbet), which is reflected in the three-sided pyramidal form of the auditorium for the "Festival du Jura." Jura's future cultural landmark is at the same time intended to sharpen perception of the extant pasture landscape of Courtemautruy by adding a new dimension.

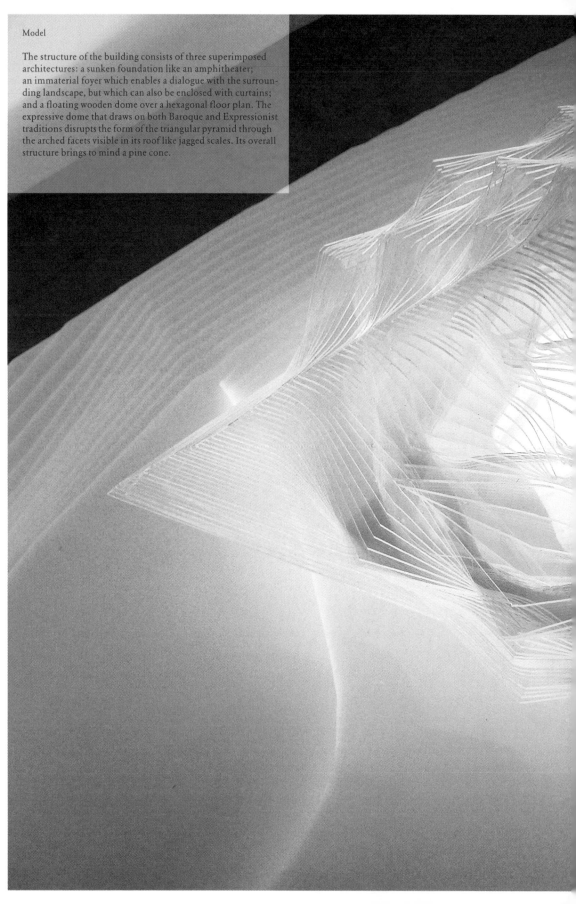

Model

The structure of the building consists of three superimposed
architectures: a sunken foundation like an amphitheater;
an immaterial foyer which enables a dialogue with the surrounding landscape, but which can also be enclosed with curtains;
and a floating wooden dome over a hexagonal floor plan. The
expressive dome that draws on both Baroque and Expressionist
traditions disrupts the form of the triangular pyramid through
the arched facets visible in its roof like jagged scales. Its overall
structure brings to mind a pine cone.

Ross Lovegrove, DNA Staircase, 2003
Lovegrove Studio, London, GB
View of Lovegrove Studio, London
....
Page 202 / 203
Detail

The DNA Staircase that Ross Lovegrove built into his
own studio in London is probably the most distinctive example
of how the designer for whom the interpretation of the
fundamentals of nature is a basic concern refers to its forms
and structure. Here it is deoxyribonucleic acid that serves
as the carrier of genetic information, thus representing
the material substance of genes. Its structure was decoded
by James Watson and Francis Crick who, together with Maurice
Wilkins, were awarded the Nobel Prize for Medicine in 1962.

Santiago Calatrava, Turning Torso, Malmö, SE, 1999–2005
Santiago Calatrava LLC, Zurich, CH
Overall view
....
Detail

Santiago Calatrava repeatedly refers to models from nature
in his buildings. The columns of the roof which spans
the platforms of Orient Station in Lisbon (1993–98) are
reminiscent of a large palm forest; and in the structure of
the station by Lyon-Satolas (1989–94), as in the mobile roof
construction for the new pavilion of the Milwaukee Art
Museum (1994–2001), birds appear to spread their wings
in flight.

In his Turning Torso skyscraper for Malmö, the light
spiral-shaped structure made up of nine separate five-story
units arranged around an access core, corresponds to the
model of a human spine with its individual vertebrae and its
capacity to combine stability and flexibility.

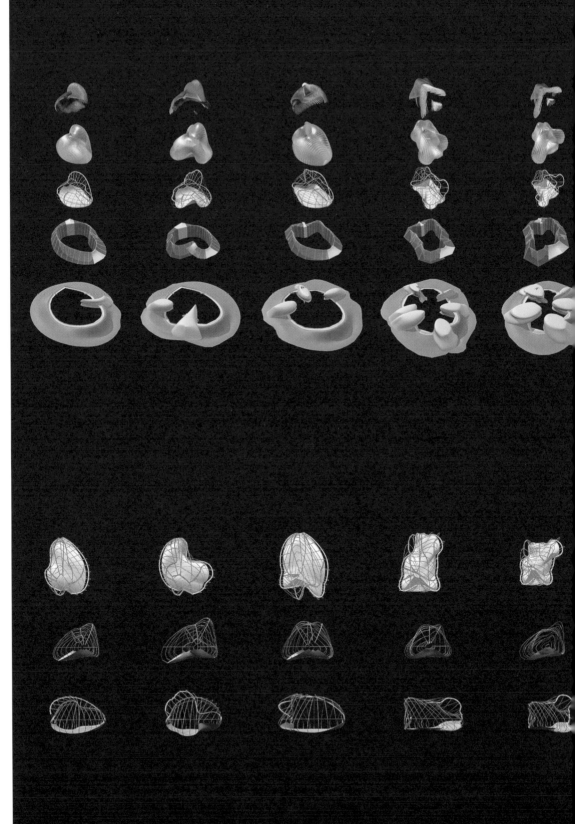

**Greg Lynn with Jeffrey Kipnis,
Embryological House, 1998–99**
Greg Lynn Form, Los Angeles, US
Exploded view
....
Structure
....
Model

Greg Lynn is regarded as one of the most important theoreticians and pioneers of blob architecture. It arose in the 1990s when the advanced CAD software provided the basis for architects to simulate natural phenomena and develop buildings with round, fluid, biomorphic forms in which the multiplicity of information malleably coalesces. This concept is well suited to the idea of growth, as embodied in Embryological House. Its structure permits endless variations and, as with the human embryo, no two specimens are ever the same. For Lynn, the transition is thereby completed from the modernist notion of a mechanical building-block system to a more vital, developing, biological model of an embryological design and its construction.

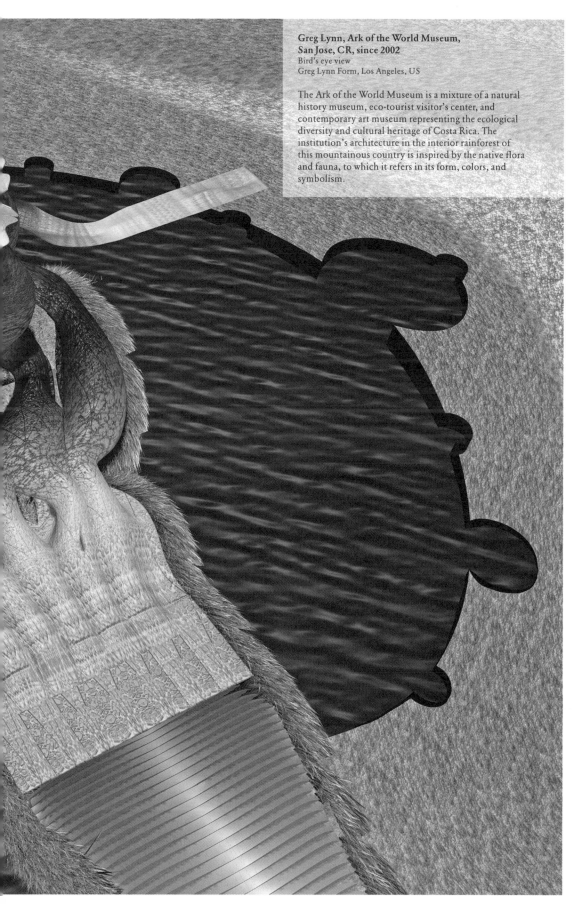

**Greg Lynn, Ark of the World Museum,
San Jose, CR, since 2002**
Bird's eye view
Greg Lynn Form, Los Angeles, US

The Ark of the World Museum is a mixture of a natural
history museum, eco-tourist visitor's center, and
contemporary art museum representing the ecological
diversity and cultural heritage of Costa Rica. The
institution's architecture in the interior rainforest of
this mountainous country is inspired by the native flora
and fauna, to which it refers in its form, colors, and
symbolism.

Future Systems, Lord's Media Centre,
Marylebone Cricket Club, London, GB, 1995–99
Future Systems, London, GB
Sketch
....
View

The Lord's Media Centre towers up behind the grandstand
of the London Marylebone Cricket Club like an abstracted
head with an oversized eye—a metaphor which seems fitting
when one considers that it is from here that the journalists
who report on the matches watch the field below.

Future Systems, with Anish Kapoor,
South Bank Centre, London, GB, 2001
Future Systems, London, GB
Photomontage
....
Model

In their unsuccessful entry for the South Bank Centre
competition, Future Systems designed a complex
of buildings with the artist Anish Kapoor which was not
intended to have the form of buildings, but rather that
of a rounded artificial hill landscape consisting of
an elevated hill for cultural uses and an oval hollow for
the commercial part of the project. This project would
have given the city on the banks of the Thames a rather
unusual accent.

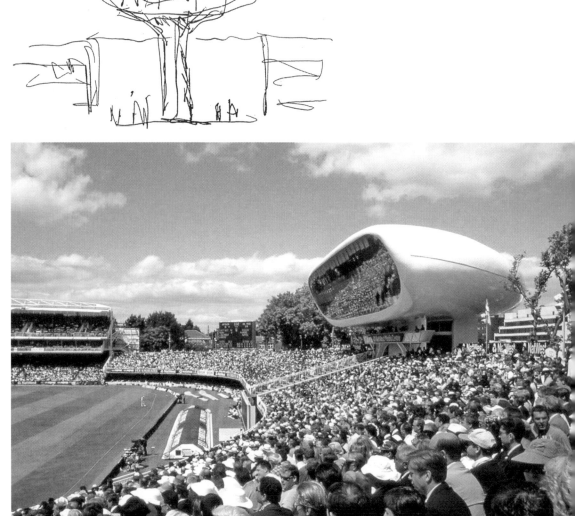

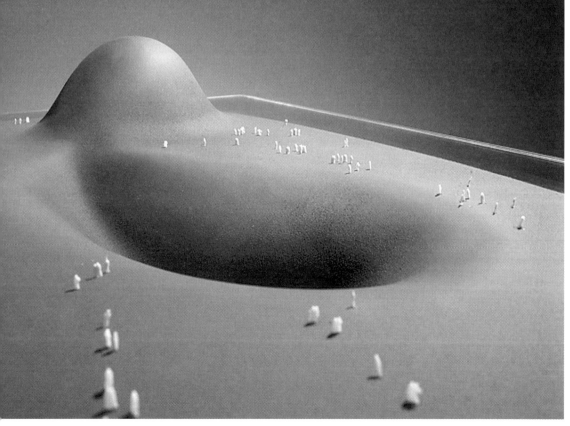

PARADISE LOST?
CONTEMPORARY STRATEGIES OF NATURE DESIGN

Angeli Sachs

In the 1952 film adaptation of Ernest Hemingway's short story *The Snows of Kilimanjaro*,[1] a successful writer and adventurer facing a life-threatening situation revisits his life in feverish and vivid dreams. This catharsis is played out against the awesome backdrop of the highest mountain in Africa (Fig. 1), the glacier-covered summit that is shown in close-up in the very first frames of the film. Just over 50 years later, in the film *An Inconvenient Truth: A Global Warning*,[2] Mount Kilimanjaro (fig. 2) offers an entirely different aspect: the majority of the ice cap has disappeared, and in all probability will be completely gone by 2020.

The 2007 Oscar-winning documentary (fig. 3) is a filmed lecture by former US Vice President Al Gore who, after his election defeat against George W. Bush, became a tireless voice in alerting the public about the consequences of global warming. Demonstrating that glacial ice is melting not only on Kilimanjaro, but also in the Alps, at the polar caps, and in Greenland, he substantiates his argument with impressive diagrams measuring man's emissions since 1958 of the carbon dioxide that is responsible for the rising temperature. Gore presents a horrific scenario of consequences for the Earth and its population: an increasing number of storms like Hurricane Katrina, which destroyed New Orleans on August 29, 2005; the dying off of the coral reefs that sustain other marine life; or a predicted six-meter rise in the sea level, resulting in the flooding of places such as the Netherlands, Florida, San Francisco Bay, and Beijing.

Any intervention in nature is Nature Design—whether it is the exploitation of raw materials, the deforestation of the rainforests, the overfishing of the seas, or any other manipulation altering natural processes. Behind these developments pushing the earth and its climate increasingly out of balance stand massive commercial interests, particularly those of the large industrialized countries which, with their perspective

1 Mount Kilimanjaro, January 1, 1950
2 Mount Kilimanjaro, February 21, 2000

skewed by self-interest, choose to ignore that they are not only robbing the poorest countries on Earth of their raw materials and prospects for the future, but, in the long run, destroying the very foundations of their own. It gives the impression of a dance on a volcano when the G8 summit in Heiligendamm in June 2007 agrees on a "climate compromise" for reducing carbon dioxide emissions in half by 2050, and limiting the rise in temperature to two degrees, yet the United States and Russia do not commit themselves to this pact of six of the other industrialized countries, and China, India, and other emerging economies register their opposition in advance. One can witness the notorious failure to implement such aims with the 2005 G8 summit in Gleneagles, where the G8 and other backers agreed to double aid to Africa by the year 2010—a goal far from becoming reality.

There is another side to Nature Design, however, which piques the interest of a design museum to explore this phenomenon: that the "model of nature" also influences the design of the human environment. This design does not only refer to the way in which people organize themselves in their given or chosen environment, or react to or protect themselves from environmental conditions, but rather that the forms, structures, and organizing principles of nature have been a constant source of inspiration in architecture and design—in some eras more notably than others.

Since the 1990s, we have witnessed a progressive return to these forms and, as we shall see, it is relevant to note that some of the most important objects were designed many decades ago. One icon of organic

3 Film poster, *An Inconvenient Truth: A Global Warning*, US, 2006

design influencing this renaissance is Alvar Aalto's Savoy Vase from 1936. While generally thought that the Finnish coastlines inspired the undulating form of the Savoy Vase and other parts of the collection **(fig. 4)**, one could also attribute these forms to anthropomorphic models or as simply an abstract expression of nature. Aalto's use of these forms in his architectural designs—by transforming, for example, his pavilion for the 1939 New York World's Fair into an "organic exhibition" **(see page 168)**—is an indication of his overall concept. Likewise iconic are Arne Jacobsen's chair designs such as the Ant (1952), Model 3107 (1955)[3]— a chair present in the millions in innumerable apartments, offices, and lecture halls—and the armchairs Swan (1957/58) and Egg (1958), which, among others, Jacobsen designed for the interior of the SAS Royal Hotel in Copenhagen **(fig. 5)**.

However, this return to the lap of nature, which itself has been so unsustainably altered, is not merely retrospective, but is also a contemporary concept. With the help of designers and architects, private living space has increasingly been transformed into a paradise, whether inspired by land or sea. Outstanding examples from the marine world **(see pages 60–79)** are Ronan and Erwan Bouroullec's Algae modules **(Fig. 6 and page 62)**, which can be arranged into complex spatial formations; Ted Muehling's designs modeled after sea snails and shells for Porzellan-Manufaktur Nymphenburg; Marcel Wanders' Foam bowl and Sponge Vase; and the Anemone and Corallo chairs by Fernando and Humberto Campana. Other designs refer to forms within a landscape, such as Zaha Hadid's Z-Scape Furniture in which—like her architecture—glaciers and

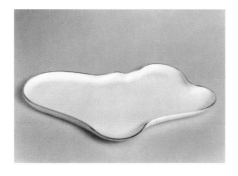

4 Alvar Aalto, "Eskimoerindens skinnbuxa" Savoy Dish, 1936
Colorless mold-blown glass with opaque white layer, 1.5 × 36.6 × 20.6 cm
Iittala oy ab, Helsinki. Museum für Gestaltung Zürich, Kunstgewerbesammlung
5 Arne Jacobsen's Swan chair in the renovated lobby of
the SAS Royal Hotel in Copenhagen, 2000

soil erosion are taken up in the flowing elements (see page 114); or Karim Rashid, who designed Ryoko perfume bottles in the form of pebbles that are soft to the touch. More common in contemporary design is an appropriation of vegetative forms (see pages 126–165), most predominantly witnessed in a return to the ornamental so vilified by Adolf Loos during the Modern movement—whether it be the tiles by BarberOsgerby for the Stella McCartney flagship stores (fig. 7 and page 154), the Dandelion lamp by Richard Hutten, the tendrils of the Heatwave radiator by Joris Laarman, the three-dimensional blossom surface of the Antibodi chaise lounge by Patricia Urquiola, or the solidified crochet flower pattern in Marcel Wanders' side table Crochet. In other designs such as Blossoms by Wieki Somers, the model becomes an object in metamorphosis. The same applies to Matali Crasset's transplant series and Ted Muehling's branch candlesticks. Anthropomorphic and zoomorphic-inspired design (see pages 190–205 and 206–227) reflects stages of development from insemination to fully-grown organisms, whether in Herzog & de Meuron's Jingzi lamp (fig. 8 and page 196), Marc Newson's Embryo Chair, Konstantin Grcic's MIURA bar stool, or Jon Male's English Hide, in which the rug spread out as a "hide" only alludes to its earlier incarnation.

But what are the reasons behind this nature-inspired design? With the exception of those who adhere to functional design, why in recent times have we started arranging ourselves in surroundings inspired by topography or vegetation, or which take on the forms of human or

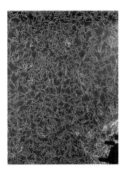

6 Ronan & Erwan Bouroullec, Algue, 2004
7 BarberOsgerby, Ceramic tiles for the Stella McCartney Flagship Stores, New York, 2002

animal bodies or body parts? What effect does this have on our positioning in our environment? In his essay, Philip Ursprung describes the use of organic forms, such as those employed by Alvar Aalto, as "ultimately anti-modern [...] as they sought their references in those forms displaced by industrialization," from which we can extract the hypothesis that forms inspired by nature become topical when modern society finds itself in crisis, and that the use of organic forms is intended to bring about harmonization and reconciliation with an external world perceived as inhospitable or hostile.

In the postwar forties, as a civilization in ruins faced reconstruction, rounded, nature-inspired forms provided a counter-image to the world of war which gave rise to such terrible destruction. This trend towards harmonization suggested an evasion of history, particularly in Germany where a sincere reconciliation with the past only began in the late sixties. At the same time, the 1972 Club of Rome report, compiled by Dennis Meadows, first raised awareness about the *Limits to Growth* within industrialized society. "The authors made clear that with continuing exponential growth the industrialized nations would lose their means of existence within the foreseeable future. The rapid reduction in supplies of raw materials, the increasing population density and worsening environmental pollution would lead to destabilization or obvious breakdown of the industrialized nations."[4]

Though published shortly before the 1973 oil crisis, this is the same message the world confronts today, now albeit in an aggravated form. The environmental movement got its start at the same time, counting

8 Herzog & de Meuron, Jingzi, 2005
9 Wieki Somers, High Tea Pot, 2003

among its important goals the resistance to nuclear energy. While the alternative concepts of this protest movement (later giving birth to the green parties) did influence product design, it is only now, thirty-five years later, that ecological awareness coupled with design is having its impact felt in lifestyle magazines, and its place on consumers' shelves. From the late seventies, design turned away from the "present" and towards an eclectic and frequently pompous Postmodernism, merging with a hedonistic lifestyle which placed *having* rather than *being* in the foreground. In retrospect, it seems like a strategy of avoidance and repression in the face of a situation in which not only the finitude of the individual but also that of his livelihood became perceptible.

The 1989 collapse of borders and the intransigent ideological divide between east and west lead to the so-called process of globalization, a reorganization of the international political and economic orders, the full consequences of which are thus far unforeseeable. And yet, in spite of the consequences and conflicts produced by globalization, climate change stands out as the most pressing crisis of global importance. Whether it is the seemingly imminent threat to our way of life, or the perceptible harbingers such as rising global temperatures and increasingly frequent natural disasters, designers are now embracing, and reconciling with, nature in shaping an artificial paradise—though not without commentary possessing an ironic or morbid undertone (fig. 9 and page 224).

Concern with nature also plays an important role in today's architecture, where these themes are often handled in a more complex way before they find their expression in design. At the same time, architecture and landscape architecture are breaching the walls that separated art and design with greater frequency. One pioneer of Nature Design in contemporary architecture is Toyo Ito with his Sendai Mediatheque (see page 244), whose interior construction was inspired by seaweed, but may also be seen as a tree structure within the otherwise almost completely transparent building. Zaha Hadid also refers to topography in many of her works in the field of architecture and design. The flowing spaces of her pavilion LFOne for the Landesgartenschau in Weil am Rhein (see page 234) are derived from "natural landscape formations such as estuaries, mountain chains, forests, deserts, gorges, drifting ice fields and seas."[5] Peter Eisenman works with concepts of physical and cultural archaeology; in developing the City of Culture of Galicia (see page 230), he employs a coding technique as a method to re-order the given context, as with DNA code. This is also the starting point for Embryological House (fig. 10 and page 256) designed by Greg Lynn with Jeffrey Kipnis. Greg Lynn is one of the most important theoreticians and pioneers of blob architecture, which arose in the 1990s as the advanced CAD software enabled architects to simulate natural phenomena and to design buildings with round, fluid, biomorphic forms in which the diversity of information flows together in a flexible manner. For Lynn, the transition from a modernist, mechanical building block system to a more vital, developing, biological model of an embryological design and its construction is thus complete. This concept is in some way analogous to Friedrich Kiesler's Endless House (see page 170) from the 1950s, which he conceived as an organism unifying all areas of life in a variable continuum.

The blob occupies perhaps a more central position in design than in architecture. The design models for the fluid and amorphous forms are to be found in the mid-twentieth century, such as with Charles and Ray Eames' La Chaise (see page 301), Arne Jacobsen's previously mentioned Egg chair, and the Phantasy Landscape by Verner Panton from 1970— though these emerged from completely different presuppositions than the computer-based blob design methods. The earliest designs that can be designated as proto-blobs are by Marc Newson, especially his Lockheed Lounge from 1986–88, constructed from aluminum sheeting. He subsequently developed the formal concept into "orgones," from which an endless series of blob objects could be derived. One of the first was the Embryo Chair (see page 197) whose organic, swollen forms perfectly

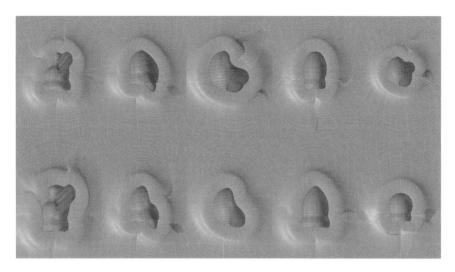

10 Greg Lynn with Jeffrey Kipnis, Embryological House, 1998–99. Nesting

embody the ideas of anthropomorphism and growth. The same form can also be carried over to other uses such as the Rock Doorstop (see page 119).[6] Another important protagonist of blob design is Karim Rashid, who is concerned with "creating a contemporary world with design" which does not only convey "the language of the digital age" but also "the new production processes and materials."[7] His first designs pointing in the direction of blob design, such as the Farrago table lamp, date—like Marc Newson's work—from the 1980s. He then designed a whole universe of objects in blob forms which range from the Garbo and Garbino wastepaper baskets (1996) to seating groups such as Pleasurescape (2001) to perfume bottles such as Ryoko for Kenzo (see .page 119).

The new manufacturing processes and materials are not only employed in blob design, but represent for the future of design one of its greatest challenges. Ross Lovegrove takes advantage of the possibilities of the digital age, and in his style takes a decisive step beyond blobism. Rather than a designer, he sees himself more as an evolutionary biologist involved through his work in the evolutionary process of reduction. This "organic essentialism" means not using more than is necessary,[8] a clue to the sustainability which should be a substantial requirement of today's design processes. The DNA Staircase (see page 250), which Ross

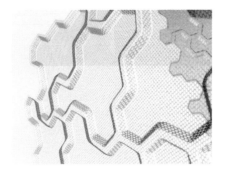
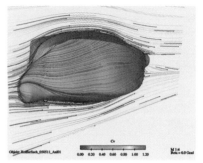

11 Werner Aisslinger, mesh – modular knitting structure, 2007
12 DaimlerChrysler, Mercedes-Benz bionic car, 2005. Measurement of aerodynamic lines
of the object boxfish

Lovegrove built into his own studio in London, is probably the most characteristic example of how the designer for whom a basic concern is examining the fundamentals of nature refers to its forms and structure. Yusuke Obuchi's Wave Garden (see page 64) is also committed to this innovative aim. The project of a wave power station for the coast of California could replace a nuclear power station near San Luis Obispo. The floating artificial landscape produces electricity by transforming the force of the Pacific waves into energy with the help of piezo-electronic sensors. When the electricity requirement is lower, the elements not in use can rise above the ocean surface and form an island that serves as a recreational landscape. Landscapes of another kind are constructed by Werner Aisslinger, who with mesh (fig. 11 and page 208) creates a modular structure from a woven honeycomb in a high-tech process, three-dimensionally formed and solidified through heating. Through endless additions they can always be formed into new organic spaces.

The basis for such developments is research in the fields of design and architecture, as well as materials research in bionics, a new transdisciplinary field of research in which the structures of nature are utilized to the benefit of technical developments. In the view of these scientists, "the range of biological construction principles and methods is the most sensible and probably also the most certain basis for the survival of our species too," particularly considering the fact that nature has a head-start of millions of years of evolutionary history during which she could "allow techniques and tools to mature into ideal forms." [9]

A good example is research in the field of current resistance. The development of the Fastskin swimsuit by Speedo for competition swimmers (see page 74) is based upon the physiognomy of the shark. The material surface of the Fastskin®FSII is like a shark's skin with its platelets of various hardness, designed of different materials for various parts of the body which reduce frictional resistance and thus enable optimum streamlining of the body in the water. These findings were transferred to the bodies of athletes and facilitated the development of the fastest swimsuit in the world. After a great deal of research, the engineers of the Mercedes-Benz bionic car, a concept vehicle from DaimlerChrysler (fig. 12 and page 78), took as their model the tropical boxfish with its angular and somewhat plump form. It has a stable and light structure combined with ideal technical qualities in currents that allow its mass to move with a minimal use of strength. This vehicle, which is the first to have been developed according to the principles of bionics, thus serves as a trailblazer for a new generation of compact cars with minimal energy consumption and greater environmental compatibility.

Another branch of research in Nature Design is biotechnology, which primarily deals with the techniques of molecular biology and genetic engineering, the latter currently the focus of considerable public attention. It not only receives inspiration from the "model of nature," but also intervenes in the structure of nature in order to manipulate it. Agriculture and medicine are important fields of application. There are various genetic engineering processes, all of which have the aim of changing the genetic information of a cell or an organism in such a way that certain qualities are strengthened or additional characteristics added. This can mean that plants are resistant to pesticides or pests, or they have increased concentrations of vitamins. In 1983, the first genetically modified tobacco plant was created; today large parts of the United States are planted with genetically modified organisms, and the same applies to parts of Canada, Argentina, Brazil, China, and India. In contrast, Europe and Japan have serious reservations. In Switzerland, after a referendum in November 2005, the use of genetic engineering in agriculture has been forbidden for an initial period of five years. The goal professed by the producers of genetically modified plants is to feed the starving world through genetic engineering, but in the worst case scenario, the manipulation of nature in the form of genetically modified

13 Cloned sheep Dolly, Edinburgh, 1997

rapeseed, soy, wheat, maize, rice, and cotton will open a Pandora's box. One of the risks is the unwanted spread of genetically modified organisms outside their areas of cultivation and the transfer of their characteristics to other plants leading to unforeseeable consequences. Potential risks including the long-term effects on the food chain are also unpredictable. An additional problem is the elimination of other species and the loss of biodiversity, primarily caused by the commercial interests of producers and suppliers of seed who are creating a cycle of dependency between genetically modified seed and pesticides, making farmers dependent on a particular type of seed as others can no longer survive in a given environment. And of course, in the age of globalization and the growing interconnectedness of market areas, these achievements are also being exported to emerging markets and the so-called Third World.

With the cloned sheep Dolly **(fig. 13)** in 1996, the possible scenarios expanded. Cloning techniques have been under development since the beginning of the 1970s, but Dolly represented the first successful cloning from the genetic material of a somatic cell of an adult mammal. The cloning of animals frequently takes place in the service of the pharmaceutical industry, where a constantly growing number of genetically engineered medicines is produced, such as against diabetes and cancer—an area of research with great potential for the future. However, with Dolly's existence the public also became aware that the cloning of people had now moved within reach, and with it all the possibilities for its abuse. A decade later we are in the midst of a discussion about designer babies. Whereas in Germany, for example, preimplantation diagnosis may only be used to find out whether an embryo has any hereditary diseases, other countries are far more permissive in their regulations. In Great Britain and Belgium, designer babies have been born who serve as cell donors for their seriously ill brothers or sisters. In Israel and also in the United States, it is permitted to determine the sex of a child through genetic selection. When will parents begin to design the child of their choice with the help of reproductive medicine? If, as an expression of a mechanical worldview, Nature Design sees life as an experimental laboratory, clear ethical lines must be drawn.

This is where the circle closes. If we were incapable of handling nature as we found it without causing lasting damage, why would we handle its manipulation any better? It seems more sensible to take inspiration from the "model of nature," with its forms, structures, and organizing principles, while respecting it so as to find innovative solutions.

1 Ernest Hemingway, *The Snows of Kilimanjaro*, Esquire, 1936. Directed by Henry King, USA, 1952.
2 *An Inconvenient Truth: A Global Warning*, directed by Davis Guggenheim, Paramount Classics and Participant Productions, USA, 2006. For further information see: www.climatecrisis.net.
3 The stacking chair 3107 is part of Series 7, which Arne Jacobsen also designed for the company Fritz Hansen following "Myren" 3100 (Ant) in 1955. Besides the stacking chairs 3107 and 3207, it includes the swivel chairs 3117 and 3217, as well as the pedestal chair 3137. The 3107 chair is among the chairs most frequently copied. See Karsten Thau and Kjeld Vindum, *Arne Jacobsen*, Copenhagen, 1998, pp. 386–96.
4 See Bernhard E. Bürdek, *Design. Geschichte, Theorie und Praxis der Produktgestaltung*, Basel, Berlin et al., 2005, p. 63. German first edition, 1991.

5 See Gordana Fontana-Giusti and Patrik Schumacher, eds., *Zaha Hadid: The Complete Works; Selected Works*, London, 2005. p. 88.
6 See Steven Skov Holt and Mara Holt Skov, *Blobjects & Beyond: The New Fluidity in Design*, San Francisco, 2005, pp. 23–41.
7 Karim Rashid in conversation with Albrecht Bangert, in *Karim Rashid – Change: Eine Design Ausstellungsreihe – Die Neue Sammlung – Design in der Pinakothek der Moderne*, exh. cat., Staatliches Museum für Angewandte Kunst Munich, Basel, Berlin et al., 2005, p. 16.
8 Ross Lovegrove in an interview with designboom, November 30, 2006, www.designboom.com.
9 See Prof. Dr. Werner Nachtigall and Kurt G. Blüchel, *Das grosse Buch der Bionik. Neue Technologien nach dem Vorbild der Natur*, Stuttgart and Munich, 2000, esp. p. 40.

SCENT

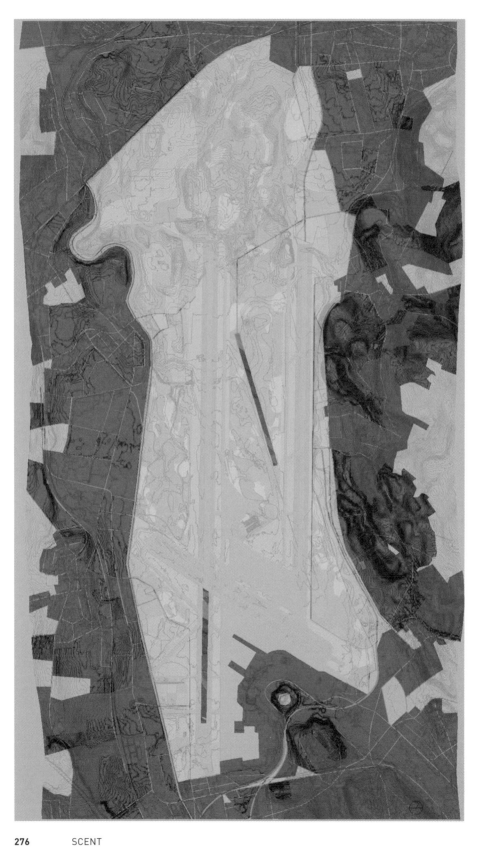

Dominique Ghiggi, *Zavana*, 2004
Computer drawings, plans, perfume
Dominique Ghiggi, Zurich, CH. Realization of the perfume:
Roman Kaiser, Director of Natural Scents, Givaudan Schweiz AG, CH

The starting point of the project is the extension of Zurich's Kloten Airport, when the removal of a landing runway between the parallel take-off runways provided new space. This reclaimed, open space is conceived as an imaginary African veldt landscape—a symbol of wilderness and freedom within the precisely defined specifications for the safety and functionality of flight operations. The urban glade is brought to life through the enhancement of its edges with a forest. It forms a contrast to the large-scale expanse of the savannah whose damp and dry grasslands are interspersed with birch and oak trees.

The creation of an atmosphere with the help of landscape architecture is comparable with the strategy of the perfume industry. Both work with an artificial nature, a new reality, through the composition of specific aromatic molecules, plants, or structures. The perfume, developed as a translation of the idea of the savannah, is a mixture of various fragrances with a clear accent on birch. Initially the scent is fresh and determined by herbal notes, later woody, exotic and warm.

Christopher Brosius, Christopher Gable, Demeter Fragrance Library, since 1993
Perfumes in glass bottles
Demeter Fragrance Library, New York, US

The fragrant worlds created by perfumeries usually pursue aims such as the accentuation of personality, the enhancement of attraction, romantic seduction, or the drowning out of bad smells by more attractive ones.

A portion of the range of scents from the Demeter Fragrance Library, of which around 200 scents are on the market, follows a different, more subversive strategy, and thoroughly overturns classical practices. "Bamboo," "Grass," "Linden," and "Ocean" may still move within the spectrum of familiar fragrances, but when "Dirt," "Earthworm," "Lobster," or "Mushroom" are found in a small scent bottle, the term *perfume* takes on a whole new meaning.

Wieki Somers, Amber, 2005
Glass, rubber, perfume, feather, various sizes, ca. 12 × 5 × 12 cm
Wieki Somers, Schiedam, NL. Realization of the perfume in
cooperation with IFF, Hilversum, NL

The three glass perfume bottles are inspired by their
model in nature—amber. The gold-yellow perfume inside is
amber in color, and is a natural resin fragrance applied to
the skin with a feather.

CLIMATE

**NOX/Lars Spuybroek with Hanna Stiller, *Joe & Joey*,
Rotterdam, NL, Competition, 1st Prize, 2006**
NOX/Lars Spuybroek, Rotterdam, NL

With *Joe & Joey,* ornament becomes structure. Conceived
as an interactive work for public space, the movement
of the sculpture is triggered by calls to two different
telephone numbers. The sculpture is modeled on several
images: a watercolor study of rocks and overgrown
ferns by John Ruskin, Logan's Rock, the human brain,
and the Wheel of Fortune. Depending on whether "Joe"
or "Joey" receives the call, the sphere changes its center
of gravity and rolls off in a different direction. Over time,
a relationship develops between "Joe" and "Joey" that
makes their reactions unpredictable for both the caller
and viewer.

NOX/Lars Spuybroek with Hanna Stiller and Beau Trincia, in cooperation with the sound artist Edwin van der Heide, Whispering Garden, Rotterdam, NL, since 2005. Competition, 1st Prize, 2005
NOX/Lars Spuybroek, Rotterdam, NL

The Whispering Garden for the Kop-van-Zuid next to Hotel New York in Rotterdam is an architectonic sculpture that reacts to the various properties—direction, force, and duration—of the frequently strong winds. Drawing upon the myths of Lorelei and the sirens, Edwin van der Heide transforms the wind into vowels sung by female voices to create a polyphonic forest of sound. The sculpture itself has its model in the arabesques into which Alphonse Maria Mucha stylized women's hair in his lithographs at the end of the nineteenth century (see page 97), translating them instead into a structure of steel and glass elements that refract the light in a full spectrum of emerald tones.

NOX/Lars Spuybroek with Hanna Stiller, Karl Rosenvinge Kjelstrup-Johnson, and Stephen Form in cooperation with Bollinger + Grohmann, Windchimes Bridge, footbridge, Zweibrüggen, DE, Competition, 1st Prize, 2006

Ruskin's Bridge, footbridge, Worrnwildnis, Kerkrade / Herzogenrath, NL and DE, Competition, 1st Prize, 2006
NOX/Lars Spuybroek, Rotterdam, NL

Windchimes Bridge is a complex and filigree structure whose elements function as wind chimes, creating sounds of varying pitch over the course of the 130-meter passage.

Ruskin's Bridge stands less for a transition than for a place in the center of the landscape. It refers to John Ruskin and his distinction between two different kinds of lines: the line of limitation and the line of force. They are echoed on the one hand in the circular form of the bridge, and on the other in the line of the ornament and the forces of nature such as the wind, the flowing of the water, and the movement of people.

Günther Vogt, *Spiegel Nebel Wind* **(Mirror Fog Wind),**
for the exhibition *Nature Design,* **Museum für Gestaltung**
Zürich, 2007
Mirror, fog machine, ventilator, and leaves
Vogt Landschaftsarchitekten AG, Zurich, CH

As we move through nature, our perception is more
complex than the visual impression we have of it. We feel
cold or heat, the humidity in the air; we absorb the smell
of plants or the earth, and hear the wide variety of sounds.
With his installation *Spiegel Nebel Wind,* Günther Vogt
does not refer to forms of nature as such, but to natural
phenomena, facilitating a physical perception of these
phenomena. The works are placed on the threshold between the exterior space of the museum and the exhibition
inside; thus, with the objects shown there focused
on visual perception, a transitional zone is created that
offers a unique experience and engenders a shift in our
perspective. In *Spiegel,* the perceived section of landscape
stands on its head; *Nebel* creates its own climatic zone;
and *Wind,* with its swirl of leaves, defines the entrance
space in a completely new way.

Megasol Solar, Solio, 2006
Solar charger for an iPod.
ABS plastic, 3.5 × 12 × 6.5 cm
Megasol Solartechnik, Aarwangen, CH

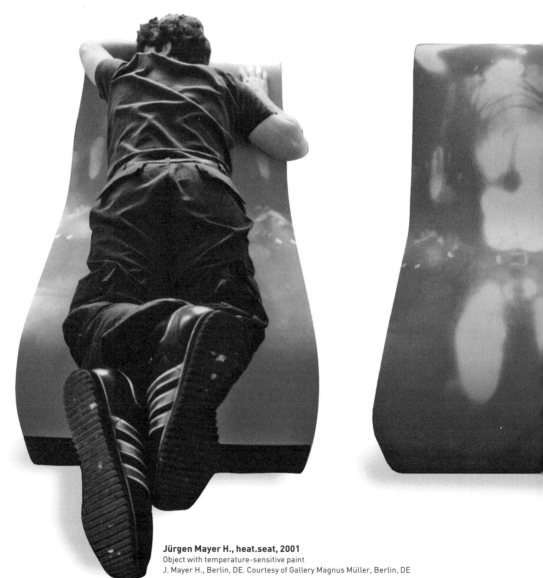

Jürgen Mayer H., heat.seat, 2001
Object with temperature-sensitive paint
J. Mayer H., Berlin, DE. Courtesy of Gallery Magnus Müller, Berlin, DE

George Nelson, Sunflower Clock, 1958
Wall clock. Birch, 75 cm
Vitra AG, Birsfelden, CH

Sharp, Sharp Elsi Mate EL-851, 1983
Solar-powered pocket calculator. Plastic, 9.5 × 6.1 cm
Sharp Corporation, JP. Museum für Gestaltung Zürich,
Designsammlung

Zaha Hadid, Patrik Schumacher,
Vortexx Chandelier, 2005
Fiberglass, auto paint, acrylic, LED, 80 × 180 cm
Sawaya & Moroni Spa, Milan, IT / Zumtobel & Staff, Dornbirn, AT

The Vortexx Chandelier is related to other furniture designs
by Zaha Hadid for Sawaya & Moroni (see page 114/115).
Its complex form flowing in arched lines follows the model
of the double helix. The beginning and end are connected
and form an endless band of light. The object takes on the
form of a star or a vortex and radiates a strong centrifugal
force. Individually programmable acrylic light spirals
are embedded in the opaque surface.

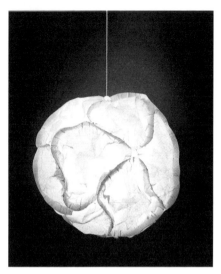

Frank Gehry, Cloud, 2005
Lamp. Connected cup-like elements made of
polyester fleece and polycarbonate, in various sizes
and variations
Belux AG, Birsfelden, CH

Susi+Ueli Berger, Wolkenlampe, 1970
Lamp. Polystyrene, 45 × 70 × 55 cm
J. Lüber, Basel, CH. Museum für Gestaltung Zürich, Designsammlung

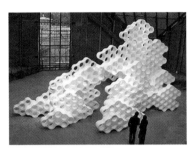

**Ronan and Erwan Bouroullec,
Cloud Modules, 2002**
Polystyrene, 105 × 187.5 × 40 cm
Cappellini, Arosio, IT

Verner Panton, Moon Lamp, 1960
Aluminum sheet, porcelain, 34.5 cm
Vitra AG, Birsfelden, CH

**Roswitha Winde-Pauls,
Tornado, 2005**
Vessel. Porcelain, hand-turned,
reductively fired, I: 51 × 23.5 cm,
II: 45 × 25 cm, III: 37.5 × 24.5 cm
Roswitha Winde-Pauls, Wotersen, DE

**Charles and Ray Eames,
La Chaise, 1948**
Chair. Two connected fiberglass bowls,
chrome, oak, 87 × 150 × 88 cm
Vitra AG, Birsfelden, CH

Ingegerd Råman, A Drop of Water, 2001
Carafe with glass. Mouth-blown
crystal glass, 24 × 10.5 cm
Orrefors, SE. Museum für Gestaltung Zürich,
Designsammlung

Luigi Colani, Drop 11.282, 1971
Tea service. Porcelain
Rosenthal AG, Selb, DE. Museum für
Gestaltung Zürich, Designsammlung

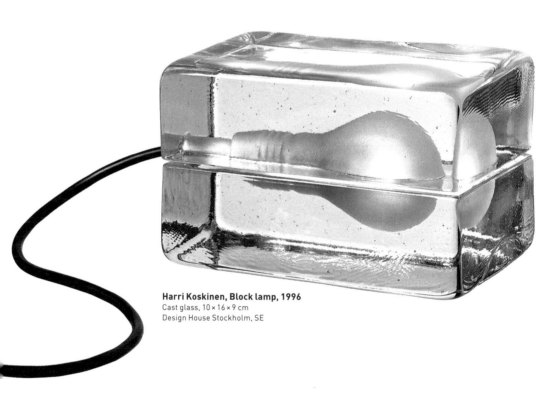

Harri Koskinen, Block lamp, 1996
Cast glass, 10 × 16 × 9 cm
Design House Stockholm, SE

Bart Lens, fool moon, 2006
Lamp. Polyethylene, steel cable, 40 × 200 cm
Eden design, Houthalen, BE

François Roche, Stéphanie Lavaux, Jean Navarro,
Water Flux (Scrambled Flat 2.0), Evolène, CH, since 2002
R&Sie(n), Paris, FR. Fondation "Maison des Alpes," CH
Cross- and longitudinal sections
Ice forms
....
Glacial cave
....
Model
....
pp. 304/305
Summer view, Winter view

Water Flux is the building design for a museum about
ice and glaciers in Valais in the Swiss Alps. Considered
a successor to Scrambled Flat—itself conceived as an
exchange between man and animal—this project works
with the various stages of ice and snow, the various
states of water and its seasonal transformations. The
digitalized structure of a traditional dwelling takes on the
form of glacial caves in its interior. The building is in a
state of exchange with the small facing lake, and inte-
grates the various stages of snowing, freezing, and thawing
so that, depending on the temperature, the façade is in a
frozen or a flowing state.

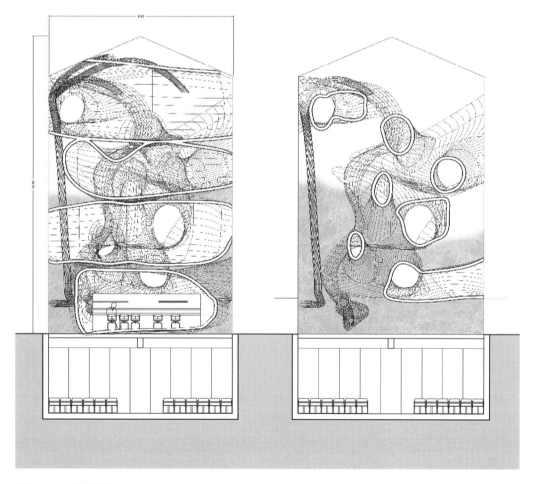

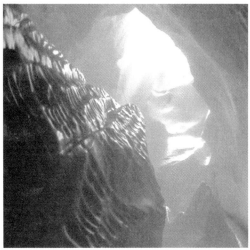
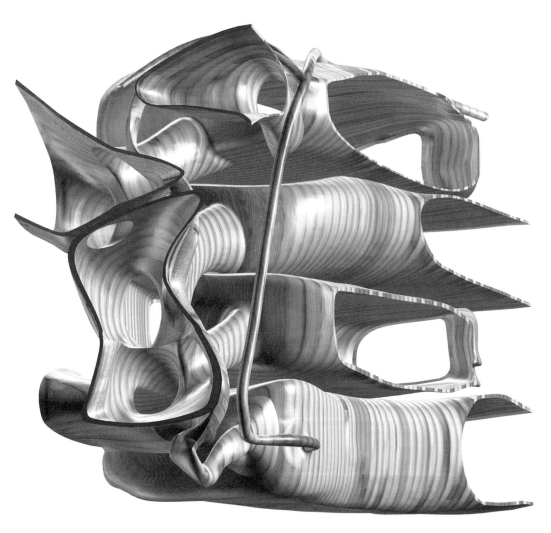

François Roche, Stéphanie Lavaux, Jean Navarro,
Pascal Bertholio, Dustyrelief /B-mu, Bangkok, TH, 2002
R&Sie(n), Paris, FR
Electrostatically-charged structure of the museum
Interior

Model of the museum covered with dust

pp. 310/311
View in urban context with polluted air

Bangkok is a rapidly-developing city full of movement
and energy, but the downside is a city with such high
air pollution that the light is tinged gray, and the region's
climate is changing. In their design for a museum for
contemporary art in Bangkok, R&Sie(n) take up these
conditions and construct the outer skin of the museum as
an electrostatically-charged aluminum shell that collects
dust particles from the air, gradually cloaking itself with
the dust of the city. The structure increasingly reflects
the energy and also the dirt of the city, forming a contrast
to the interior of the museum, which is conceived as a
timeless white cube. The dust façade is of great aesthetic
appeal, but concentrates within itself the whole horror
of a threatened and polluted environment.

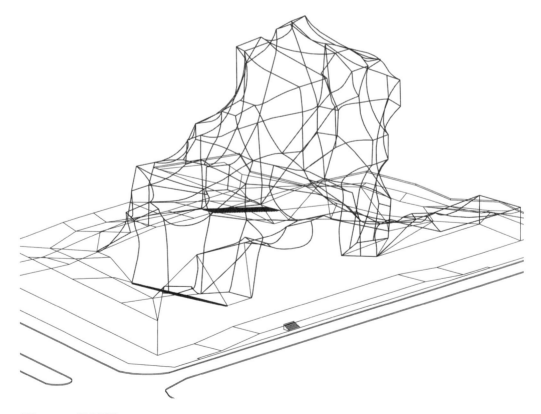

AUTHOR BIOGRAPHIES

Barry Bergdoll

Philip Johnson Chief Curator of Architecture and Design at the Museum of Modern Art and Professor of Modern Architectural History at Columbia University. Holding a B.A. from Columbia, an M.A. from King's College, Cambridge, and a Ph.D. from Columbia, his broad interests center on modern architectural history with a particular emphasis on France and Germany since 1800.

Bergdoll has organized, curated, and consulted on many landmark exhibitions of nineteenth- and twentieth-century architecture including *Mies in Berlin* at MoMA (2001), with Terence Riley; *Breuer in Minnesota* at the Minneapolis Institute of Arts (2002); *Les Vaudoyer: Une Dynastie d'Architectes at the Musée d'Orsay*, Paris (1991); and *Ste. Geneviève/Pantheon, Symbol of Revolutions* at the Canadian Centre for Architecture, Montreal (1989).

He is author or editor of numerous publications including *Mies in Berlin* (winner of the 2002 Philip Johnson Award of the Society of Architectural Historians and AICA Best Exhibition Award, 2002); *Karl Friedrich Schinkel: An Architecture for Prussia* (1994), winner of the AIA Book Award in 1995; and *European Architecture 1750–1890,* in the Oxford History of Art series. An edited volume, *Fragments: Architecture and the Unfinished,* was recently published by Thames & Hudson, London 2006.

He serves currently as President of the Society of Architectural Historians.

Dario Gamboni

Professor of Art History (Modern and Contemporary Art and Architecture) at the University of Geneva (since 2004), previously at the University of Lyon II (1991–97), at Case Western Reserve University, Cleveland, Ohio (1998–2000), and at the University of Amsterdam (2001–04). Member of the Institut Universitaire de France (1993–98), Ailsa Mellon Bruce Fellow at the Center of Advanced Study in the Visual Arts, National Gallery of Art, Washington, D.C. (1996), Meret Oppenheim Award 2006. Visiting professor at Strasbourg, Frankfurt am Main, Buenos Aires, Freiburg im Breisgau, and Mexico.

Publications in book form: *Un iconoclasme moderne. Théorie et pratiques contemporaines du vandalisme artistique,* Lausanne and Zürich, 1983; *Louis Rivier (1885–1963) et la peinture religieuse en Suisse romande,* Lausanne, 1985; *La géographie artistique* (Ars helvetica, vol. I), Disentis, 1987; *La plume et le pinceau. Odilon Redon et la literature,* Paris, 1989; *Zeichen der Freiheit. Das Bild der Republik in der Kunst des 16. bis 20. Jahrhunderts,* ed. with Georg Germann, Bern, 1991; *The Destruction of Art: Iconoclasm and Vandalism since the French Revolution,* New Haven and London, 1997; *Odilon Redon, Das Faß Amontillado. Der Traum eines Traumes,* Frankfurt am Main, 1998; *Crises de l'image religieuse / Krisen religiöser Kunst,* ed. with Olivier Christin, Paris, 2000; *Potential Images: Ambiguity and Indeterminacy in Modern Art,* London 2002.

Angeli Sachs

Studied art history, German and sociology at the Universities of Augsburg and Frankfurt am Main. Since 2006 is Head of Exhibitions at the Museum für Gestaltung Zürich (Museum of Design Zurich). Previously Editor-in-Chief for Architecture and Design, Prestel Publishing, Munich (2001–05), Academic Assistant at the Institute for History and Theory of Architecture (gta), Swiss Federal Institute of Technology (ETH) in Zürich (1995–2000), freelance academic work for the German Architecture Museum, Frankfurt am Main (1994–95), and Press Officer for the Frankfurter Kunstverein (1990–93).

Numerous exhibitions and publications on architecture and art of the twentieth and twenty-first century, including: *Museums for a new Millennium: Concepts, Projects, Buildings* (with Vittorio Magnago Lampugnani), Munich, 1999; *Minimal Architecture* (with Ilka & Andreas Ruby, Philip Ursprung), Munich, 2003, and *Jewish Identity in Contemporary Architecture* (with Edward van Voolen), Munich, 2004.

Philip Ursprung

Studied art history, history, and German literature in Geneva, Vienna, and Berlin, receiving a PhD from the Freie Universität Berlin in 1993. He wrote his Habilitation at the Swiss Federal Institute of Technology (ETH) in Zurich in 1999. Ursprung has taught art history at the Universities of Geneva, Basel, and Zurich, at the Swiss Federal Institute of Technology, (ETH) in Zürich, at the Kunsthochschule Berlin-Weissensee, and at the Universität der Künste Berlin. From 2001 to 2005 he was Science Foundation Professor for Art History in the Department of Architecture at ETH Zürich. Since 2005 he is Professor for Modern and Contemporary Art at the University of Zurich. In 2007, he was visiting professor at the Graduate School of Architecture, Planning and Preservation of Columbia University New York.

He was a curator at the Kunsthalle Palazzo, Liestal, Switzerland; a visiting curator at the Museum of Contemporary Art in Basel; the Canadian Centre for Architecture in Montréal; and at the Graduate School of Architecture, Planning and Preservation of Columbia University, New York.

Publications include: *Grenzen der Kunst: Allan Kaprow und das Happening, Robert Smithson und die Land Art,* Munich, 2003; *Minimal Architecture* (with Ilka & Andreas Ruby and Angeli Sachs), Munich, 2003; *Images: A Picture Book of Architecture* (with Ilka & Andreas Ruby), Munich, 2004; *Pictures of Architecture, Architecture of Pictures: A Conversation by Jacques Herzog and Jeff Wall,* moderated by Philip Ursprung, Vienna, 2004; and as editor: *Herzog & de Meuron: Natural History,* exh. cat., Canadian Centre for Architecture Montreal, Baden, 2002.

BIBLIOGRAPHY

General

Becker, Peter René, *nestWerk: Architektur und Lebewesen,* ed. Horst Braun, exh. cat., Übersee-Museum Bremen, Oldenburg, 2001.

Betsky, Aaron, and Adam Eeuwens, *False Flat: Why Dutch Design Is so Good,* London, 2004.

Blüchel, Kurt G., and Fredmund Malik, eds., *Faszination Bionik. Die Intelligenz der Schöpfung,* Munich, 2006.

Bürdek, Bernhard E., *Design. Geschichte, Theorie und Praxis der Produktgestaltung,* Basel et al, 2005. German first edition, 1991.

Faass, Martin, *Natur ganz Kunst. Positionen zeitgenös-sischer Gestaltung,* exh. cat., Museum für Kunst und Gewerbe, Hamburg, 2004.

Fahr-Becker, Gabriele, *Jugendstil,* Königswinter, 2004.

Fiell, Charlotte & Peter, *Design des 20. Jahrhunderts,* Cologne, 2000.

Fiell, Charlotte & Peter, *Scandinavian Design / Skandinavisches Design,* Cologne, 2002.

Frampton, Kenneth, *Modern Architecture,* London, 1980.

Jodidio, Philip, *Architecture: Nature,* Munich et al, 2006.

Klanten, Robert, et al, eds., *Into the Nature: Of Creatures and Wilderness,* Berlin, 2006.

Lupton, Ellen, *Skin: Surface, Substance + Design,* exh. cat., Cooper-Hewitt National Design Museum, Smithsonian Institution, New York, 2003.

Lupton, Ellen, et al, *Inside Design Now: National Design Triennial,* exh. cat., Cooper-Hewitt National Design Museum, Smithsonian Institution, New York, 2003.

Nachtigall, Werner, and Kurt G. Blüchel, *Das große Buch der Bionik. Neue Technologien nach dem Vorbild der Natur,* Stuttgart and Munich, 2000.

Non-standard architectures, ed. Fréderic Migayrou and Zeynep Mennan, exh. cat., Centre Pompidou, Paris, 2004.

Pevsner, Nikolaus, *Pioneers of Modern Movement,* London, 1936. Later published as *Pioneers of Modern Design: From William Morris to Walter Gropius,* New York, 1949.

Powers, Alan, *Natur und Design. Inspirationen für Architektur, Mode und angewandte Kunst,* Bern et al, 2000.

Ramakers, Renny, ed., *simply droog: 10 + 1 years of avant-garde design from the Netherlands,* Amsterdam, 2004.

Ruby, Ilka & Andreas, and Philip Ursprung, *Images: A Picture Book of Architecture,* Munich et al, 2004.

Ruby, Ilka & Andreas, Angeli Sachs and Philip Ursprung, *Minimal Architecture,* Munich et al, 2003.

Schmidt, Petra, et al, eds., *Patterns. Muster in Design, Kunst und Architektur,* Basel et al, 2005.

Skov Holt, Steven, and Mara Holt Skov, *Blobjects & Beyond: The New Fluidity in Design,* San Francisco, 2005.

Sterner, Gabriele, *Jugendstil. Kunstformen zwischen Individualismus und Massengesellschaft,* Cologne, 1975.

Theater der Natur und Kunst. Wunderkammern des Wissens, ed. Horst Bredekamp, exh. cat., Humboldt-Universität zu Berlin im Martin-Gropius-Bau, 2 Bde., Berlin, 2000.

The Origin of Things: Sketches, Models, Prototypes, ed. Thimo Te Duits, exh. cat., Museum Boijmans Van Beuningen, Rotterdam, 2003.

Alvar Aalto

Alvar Aalto: Between Humanism and Materialism, ed. Peter Reed, exh. cat., The Museum of Modern Art, New York, New York, 1998.

Alvar & Aino Aalto, Design: Collection Bischofberger, ed. Thomas Kellein, exh. cat., Kunsthalle Bielefeld, Ostfildern-Ruit, 2004.

Weston, Richard, *Alvar Aalto,* London, 1995.

Karl Blossfeldt

Blossfeldt, Karl, *Urformen der Kunst. Wundergarten der Natur. Das fotografische Werk in einem Band,* Munich et al, 1994. First editions: *Urformen der Kunst,* Berlin, 1928; *Wundergarten der Natur,* Berlin, 1932.

Lammert, Angela, ed., *Konstruktionen von Natur. Von Blossfeldt zur Virtualität,* Akademie der Künste, Berlin, Dresden, 2001.

Meyer Stump, Ulrike, "Modelle einer verborgenen Geometrie der Natur: Karl Blossfeldts Meurer-Bronzen" in: *Herzog & de Meuron: Natural History,* ed. Philip Ursprung, exh. cat., Canadian Centre for Architecture, Montréal, Baden, 2002, pp. 312–19.

Ronan and Erwan Bouroullec

Ronan and Erwan Bouroullec, London, 2003.

R. Buckminster Fuller

Your Private Sky: R. Buckminster Fuller; Design Art Science, ed. Joachim Krausse and Claude Lichtenstein, exh. cat., Museum für Gestaltung Zürich, Baden, 1999.

Colani

Bangert, Albrecht, ed., *Colani. Das Gesamtwerk,* Schopfheim, 2004.

Charles Darwin

Bredekamp, Horst, *Darwins Korallen. Frühe Evolutions-modelle und die Tradition der Naturgeschichte,* Berlin, 2005.

Darwin, Charles, *On the Origin of Species by Means of Natural Selection, or the Preservation of Favoured Races in the Struggle for Life,* London, 1859.

Peter Eisenman
Peter Eisenman. *Barfuss auf weiss glühenden Mauern /*
Barefoot on White-Hot Walls, ed. Peter Noever, exh. cat.,
MAK Wien, Ostfildern-Ruit, 2004.

Olafur Eliasson
Eliasson, Olafur, *Your Engagement has Consequences:*
On the Reality of Your Reality, Baden, 2006.

Grynsztejn, Madeleine, et al, *Olafur Eliasson*, London, 2002.

Future Systems
Future Systems, *Unique Building: Lord's Media Centre*,
Chichester, 2001.

Sudjic, Deyan, *Future Systems*, London, 2006.

Johann Wolfgang von Goethe
von Goethe, Johann Wolfgang, *Die Metamorphose der*
Pflanzen, Ettinger, Gotha, 1790. Ed. Junk, Berlin 1924,
with original artwork, ed. Julius Schuster.

von Goethe, Johann Wolfgang, *Werke. Hamburger*
Ausgabe in 14 Bänden, vol. 1, *Gedichte und Epen*, Hamburg,
1948–1960, pp. 199–201.

von Goethe, Johann Wolfgang, *Werke. Hamburger Ausgabe*
in 14 Bänden, vol. 13, *Naturwissenschaftliche Schriften I*,
Hamburg, 1948–1960, pp. 64–101.

Konstantin Grcic
Böhm, Florian, ed., *KGID Konstantin Grcic Industrial Design*,
London, 2005.

MIURA stool, designed by Konstantin Grcic, photographed
by Florian Böhm, NYC 2006, Plank Collezioni Srl, Ora, 2007.

Zaha Hadid
Architecture of Zaha Hadid in Photographs by Hélène Binet,
Baden, 2000.

Fontana-Giusti, Gordana, and Patrik Schumacher,
eds., *Zaha Hadid: The Complete Works*, 4 vols., London,
2005.

Zaha Hadid, exh. cat., Solomon R. Guggenheim Museum,
New York, 2006.

Zaha Hadid: Architektur / Architecture, ed. Peter Noever,
exh. cat., MAK Wien, Ostfildern-Ruit, 2003.

Ernst Haeckel
Breidbach, Olaf, *Ernst Haeckel. Bildwelten der Natur*,
Prestel, Munich et al, 2006.

Haeckel, Ernst, *Kunstformen aus dem Meer.*
Der Radiolarien-Atlas von 1862, Munich et al, 2005.

Haeckel, Ernst, *Kunstformen der Natur*, Munich and
New York, 1998. First edition: Bibliographisches Institut,
Leipzig and Vienna, 1904.

Serge Hasenböhler
Wittwer, Hans-Peter, ed., *Serge Hasenböhler. Album*,
Zurich, 2006.

Herzog & de Meuron
Ursprung, Philip, *Herzog & de Meuron: Natural History*,
exh. cat., Canadian Centre for Architecture, Montréal,
Baden, 2002.

Alexander von Humboldt
von Humboldt, Alexander, *Kosmos, Entwurf einer*
physischen Weltbeschreibung, 5 vols., Cotta, Stuttgart,
Tübingen, 1845–1862. Reprint: Frankfurt am Main, 2004.

Toyo Ito
Witte, Ron, ed., *CASE: Toyo Ito, Sendai Mediatheque*,
Harvard University Graduate School of Design, Munich
et al, 2002.

Arne Jacobsen
Thau, Karsten, and Kjeld Vindum, *Arne Jacobsen*,
Copenhagen, 1998.

Hella Jongerius
Schouwenberg, Louise, *Hella Jongerius*, London, 2003.

Friedrich Kiesler
Bogner, Dieter, *Friedrich Kiesler 1890–1965: Inside the*
Endless House, exh. cat., Historisches Museum der Stadt
Wien, Vienna, 1997.

Bogner, Dieter, and Peter Noever, *Frederick J. Kiesler:*
Endless Space, exh. cat., MAK Center for Art and
Architecture, Los Angeles, Ostfildern-Ruit, 2000.

Frederick Kiesler. Artiste-architecte, exh. cat.,
Centre Georges Pompidou, Paris, 1996.

Friedrich Kiesler: Endless House, 1947–1961,
Ostfildern-Ruit, 2003.

Kisho Kurokawa
Kisho Kurokawa, Metabolism and Symbiosis / Metabolismus
und Symbiosis, ed. Peter Cachola Schmal et al, exh. cat.,
Deutsches Architektur Museum, Frankfurt am Main,
Berlin, 2005.

Ross Lovegrove
supernatural: The Work of Ross Lovegrove, London, 2004.

Greg Lynn
Lynn, Greg, *Animate Form*, New York, 1999.

Lynn, Greg, *Architecture for an Embryological Housing*,
New York, 2002.

Jürgen Mayer H.
J. Mayer H., Metropol Parasol: Redesigning of Plaza de la
Encarnación in Sevilla, ed. Andres Lepik, exh. cat., Kunst-
bibliothek, Staatliche Museen zu Berlin, Berlin, 2005.

Activators_J. Mayer H. / Germany, DD 19, Design Document
Series, Seoul, 2006.

Olaf Nicolai
Olaf Nicolai 2003–06, exh. cat., Galerie EIGEN + ART,
Leipzig and Nuremberg, 2006.

Pfleger, Susanne and Olaf Nicolai, eds., *rewind forward*,
Ostfildern-Ruit, 2003.

NOX / Lars Spuybroek
Spuybroek, Lars, *Machining Architecture:
NOX*, London, 2004.

Tramontin, Maria Ludovica, *nox*, Rome, 2006.

Frei Otto
*Frei Otto. Das Gesamtwerk. Leicht bauen, natürlich gestal-
ten*, ed. Winfried Nerdinger, exh. cat., Architekturmuseum
der TU München in der Pinakothek der Moderne, Basel
et al, 2005.

Karim Rashid
Karim Rashid – Change, Eine Ausstellungsreihe der
Neuen Sammlung – Staatliches Museum für Angewandte
Kunst / Design in der Pinakothek der Moderne, Munich,
Basel et al, 2005.

R&Sie(n)
Corrupted Biotopes_R&Sie... architects / France,
DD 5, Design Document Series, Seoul, 2004.

Lan, Bruce Q, ed., *R&Sie(n): I've heard about…(c)
a flat fat growing urban experiment*, Beijing, 2006.

Ruby, Andreas and Benoît Durandin, eds., *R&Sie…
architects: Spoiled Climate*, Basel, 2004.

Hans Scharoun
Kirschenmann, Jörg C., and Eberhard Syring, *Hans
Scharoun: die Forderung des Unvollendeten*, Stuttgart, 1993.

Schirren, Matthias, "Kunst und Natur in der Architektur
der Moderne. Anmerkungen zu einer Wahlverwandt-
schaft" in: *Konstruktionen von Natur. Von Blossfeldt zur
Virtualität*, ed. Angela Lammert, exh. cat., Akademie
der Künste, Berlin, Dresden, 2001, pp. 151–164.

Bruno Taut
Nerdinger, Winfried, et al, *Bruno Taut, 1880–1938. Architekt
zwischen Tradition und Avantgarde*, Stuttgart and Munich,
2001.

Schirren, Matthias, "Kunst und Natur in der Architektur
der Moderne. Anmerkungen zu einer Wahlverwandt-
schaft" in: *Konstruktionen von Natur. Von Blossfeldt zur
Virtualität*, ed. Angela Lammert, exh. cat., Akademie
der Künste, Berlin, Dresden, 2001, pp. 151–64.

Schirren, Matthias, *Bruno Taut. Alpine Architektur.
Eine Utopie / A Utopia*, Munich et al, 2004.

Thiekötter, Angelika, et al, *Kristallisationen, Splitterungen.
Bruno Tauts Glashaus*, exh. cat., Werkbund-Archiv
im Martin-Gropius-Bau, Berlin, Basel et al, 1993.

Günther Vogt
Vogt, Günther, *Miniature and Panorama: Vogt Landscape
Architects, Works 2000–06*, Baden, 2006.

Christian Waldvogel
Waldvogel, Christian, *Globus Cassus*, Bundesamt
für Kultur, Baden, 2004.

Marcel Wanders
Wanders, Marcel, *Wanders Wonders: Design for a New Age*,
exh. cat., Het Kruithuis Museum of Contemporary Art,
's-Hertogenbosch, Rotterdam, 1999.

ILLUSTRATION CREDITS

© 2007, Prolitteris, 8033 Zürich

pp. 254, 255: Calatrava, Santiago
pp. 204, 205: Goulet, Olivier
pp. 6, 7: Hasenböhler, Serge
p. 220/221: Nicolai, Olaf
p. 302: Råman, Ingegerd
pp. 122/123, 124, 125: Waldvogel, Christian
p. 141: Lalique, René
pp. 96, 97: Mucha, Alphonse Maria
pp. 44, 45: Scharoun, Hans
pp. 36, 37, 85: van de Velde, Henry

pp. 14–16, 23–25: Franz Xaver Jaggy © ZHdK
pp. 18, 19: Regula Bearth © ZHdK
p. 26/27: Betty Fleck © ZHdK
pp. 28/29, 30/31: Regula Bearth © ZHdK
pp. 34–37: Franz Xaver Jaggy © ZHdK
p. 48, fig. 1: © Jörg P. Anders
p. 49, fig. 3: from: Kenneth P. Hazlett, et al, eds., *Collection of Architectural Designs: including designs which have been executed and objects whose execution was intended by Karl Friedrich Schinkel*, Guildford, 1989.
p. 52, fig. 4: from: *Pierre A. Frey, E. Viollet-le-Duc et le Massif du Mont-Blanc*, Lausanne, 1988.
p. 53, figs. 5, 6: from: Wim de Wit, ed., *Louis Sullivan: The Function of Ornament*, New York, 1986.
p. 56, fig. 7: © Cervin Robinson. From: Wim de Wit, ed., *Louis Sullivan: The Function of Ornament*, New York, 1986.
p. 56, fig. 8: from: *Ernst Haeckel: Kunstformen aus dem Meer*, Munich, 2005.
p. 68 top: Marlen Perez © ZHdK
p. 68 bottom: Franz Xaver Jaggy © ZHdK
pp. 70 top left, 71 top right: © Maarten van Houten
pp. 70 bottom, 74 top right: Regula Bearth © ZHdK
p. 76: © Miles Butterworth
p. 78 bottom: Franz Xaver Jaggy © ZHdK
p. 82: Franz Xaver Jaggy © ZHdK
p. 86: Marlen Perez © ZHdK
p. 87: Betty Fleck © ZHdK
p. 88/89: Marlen Perez © ZHdK
p. 102, fig. 3: From: Nancy Mowll Mathews, *Paul Gauguin: An Erotic Life*, Yale, 2001.
p. 102, fig. 4: From: Philippe Garner, *Emile Gallé*, Paris, 1977.
p. 102, fig. 6: © Bildarchiv Photo Marburg, neg. 419-48
p. 104, figs. 7–9: Dario Gamboni
p. 106, fig. 10: Archive Dario Gamboni
p. 106, fig. 12: From: Guy Cogeval et al, *Edouard Vuillard*, New Haven, 2003.
p. 108, fig. 14: Dario Gamboni
p. 108, fig. 15 © Guimard Hector, © Estate Brassaï – RMN; from: *Minotaure* (N° 3–4), Paris, 1933.
p. 117: © Maarten van Houten
p. 118: Franz Xaver Jaggy © ZHdK
p. 138 bottom: Marlen Perez © ZHdK
p. 139: © Patrick Gries
p. 141 top left: Marlen Perez © ZHdK
p. 141 top right: © Stefan Kirchner
p. 141 bottom: Franz Xaver Jaggy © ZHdK
pp. 144/145, 147: © David Franck
p. 150/151: Regula Bearth © ZHdK
p. 156 top left: Franz Xaver Jaggy © ZHdK
p. 158 center left: Franz Xaver Jaggy © ZHdK
p. 168/169: Ezra Stoller © Esto
p. 174/175: © SV-Bilderdienst, Bild Nr. 00136853

p. 181, figs. 1, 2: Ezra Stoller © Esto
p. 182, fig. 3: From: Henry Moore, *Henry Moore Plastiken 1912–80*. Stuttgart, 1981.
p. 183, figs. 4, 5: From: James D. Watson, *The Double Helix*, New York, 1968.
p. 186, fig. 8: From: Joachim Krausse, Claude Lichtenstein, ed., *Your Private Sky: R. Buckminster Fuller*, Baden, 1999.
p. 186, fig. 9: © Werek, 1972, SV-Bilderdienst, Fig. 00051202
p. 189, fig. 11: From: David Stravitz, *The Chrysler Building: Creating a New York Icon*, New York, 2002.
p. 198 top right: © Riccardo Bianchi
p. 198 center left: Franz Xaver Jaggy © ZHdK
p. 198 center right: Betty Fleck © ZHdK
pp. 200, 201, 212, 213: Franz Xaver Jaggy © ZHdK
p. 216 top right: Betty Fleck © ZHdK
p. 216 center right: Franz Xaver Jaggy © ZHdK
p. 219: © Maarten van Houten
p. 223: Franz Xaver Jaggy © ZHdK
pp. 234, 235, 237: © Hélène Binet
pp. 238 bottom, 239: © Roland Halbe
pp. 244, 245: © Nacasa & Partners
p. 246/247: © Herzog & de Meuron
pp. 254, 255: © Oliver Schuh, Palladium Photodesign, Köln, DE
p. 263, fig. 1: © Frederic Lewis, 1/1/1950, Getty Images, Fig. 52260745
p. 263, fig. 2: http://svs.gsfc.nasa.gov/vis/a000000/a002700/a002701/index.html
p. 264, fig. 3: http://www.climatecrisis.net/downloads/images/poster.jpg
p. 265, fig. 4: Marlen Perez © ZHdK
p. 265, fig. 5: From: Brochure, *40th anniversary of the Royal Hotel Copenhagen*, Copenhagen, 2000.
p. 269, fig. 10: Greg Lynn Form, Los Angeles, US
p. 272, fig. 13: © AP, 12/31/1997, SV-Bilderdienst, Fig. 00129764
pp. 282, 283: © Elian Somers
p. 294 top: Regula Bearth © ZHdK
pp. 295 bottom, p. 298 bottom: Franz Xaver Jaggy © ZHdK
p. 301 center: © Bernd Perlbach
p. 302 center: Franz Xaver Jaggy © ZHdK

We would like to thank all the architects, designers and artists, as well as the mentioned firms, collections, and private owners for kindly providing us with illustrative material.

We have taken great pains to locate all copyright holders. Should we have been unsuccessful in individual cases, copyright claims should be addressed to the Museum für Gestaltung Zürich.

Index

italic = images

NATURE DESIGN
From Inspiration to Innovation

Exhibition and Publication
by the Museum für Gestaltung Zürich
Christian Brändle, Director

Curator: Angeli Sachs

Publication
Concept, Texts: Angeli Sachs
Editing: Christina Reble, Angeli Sachs
Editorial Assistance and Image research:
Nava Sutter, Marilena Cipriano, Rebecca Heil
Design: Lars Müller and Esther Schütz,
Integral Lars Müller
Copyediting: Jonathan Fox
Translation from the German:
James Roderick O'Donovan, Steve Gander
Repro: SRS Medien, Hohberg-Hofweier
Printing and Binding: Kösel, Altusried-Krugzell

© 2007
Zürcher Hochschule der Künste ZHdK,
Zürcher Fachhochschule
and Lars Müller Publishers

Museum für Gestaltung Zürich
Ausstellungsstrasse 60
CH-8005 Zürich / Switzerland
www.museum-gestaltung.ch

Lars Müller Publishers
CH-5400 Baden / Switzerland
www.lars-muller-publishers.com

ISBN 978-3-03778-098-5

For their generous support,
special thanks to